SAY IT

WITH

confidence

Overcome the Mental Blocks That Keep You from Making Great Presentations & Speeches

---

MARGOT KRASNE

WARNER BOOKS

A Time Warner Company

Grateful acknowledgment is given to reprint from the following:

Abnormal Psychology and Modern Life by Robert Carson and James Butcher. Copyright © 1992 by HarperCollins Publishers, Inc. Reprinted by permission of Addison-Wesley Educational Publishers, Inc.

David G. Myers, *Psychology,* 3rd edition, Worth Publishers, New York, 1992. Reprinted with permission.

Carl Goldberg, *Understanding Shame,* Jason Aronson, New Jersey, 1991. Reprinted with permission.

The Interpersonal World of the Infant by Daniel N. Stern. Copyright © 1987 by Basic Books, Inc. Reprinted with permission of HarperCollins Publishers, Inc.

The Estate of Margery Williams for permission to quote from *The Velveteen Rabbit* under the condition that it be stated that Margery Williams's intent was to speak about a child and his toy and not about a parent's love for a child.

For the definitions *sell* and *persuade:* Adapted and reproduced by permission from *The American Heritage Dictionary of the English Language,* 3rd edition. Copyright © 1992 by Houghton Mifflin Company.

For the definitions *shame* and *sell: The Compact Edition of the Oxford English Dictionary.* Oxford University Press, 1985, by permission of Oxford University Press.

For the definition *shame*: Reprinted with the permission of Pocket Books, a Division of Simon & Schuster, from *Langenscheidt's German-English Dictionary* by K. G. Langenscheidt. Copyright © 1952, 1969, 1970, 1993 by Langenscheidt KG, Berlin and Munich, Germany.

For the definitions *improve, misconception, professional, sell,* and *strategy: The Random House Dictionary of the English Language, The Unabridged Edition.* Jess Stein, ed. Copyright © 1967 by Random House, Inc. Reprinted by permission of Random House, Inc.

For the definitions *cybernetics* and *misconception: Webster's New Universal Unabridged Dictionary,* Barnes & Noble Books, 1994.

Warner Books, Inc., 1271 Avenue of the Americas, New York, NY 10020

Visit our Web site at http://warnerbooks.com

⚏ A Time Warner Company

Printed in the United States of America
First Printing: September 1997
10 9 8 7 6 5 4 3

Library of Congress Cataloging-in-Publication Data

Krasne, Margo T.
    Say it with confidence : overcome the mental blocks that keep you
from making great presentations and speeches / Margo T. Krasne.
      p. cm.
    ISBN 0-446-67288-2
    1. Business presentations. 2. Public speaking. I. Title.
HF5718.22.K73 1997
658.4'5—dc20   96-9246
                                                   CIP

Book design and composition by L&G McRee
Cover design © Irving Freeman Design Co. 1997

To my mother who I'm sure is smiling.

Acknowledgments

I began this book six years ago, because a number of people told me that a book brings in business. That's how it started, but that was not what kept me going through the tortuous work and numerous rejections, even as the business thrived—leaving the original raison d'être without a raison d'être. What kept me at it was the unerring faith of a special few, the realization somewhere in the fourth year that the book was actually wanted and, more importantly, needed, and the incredible education I received as I exposed my writing and thinking to others' scrutiny.

I had decided early on to limit the working critics to a few people—an incredibly selfish but necessary decision—necessary, because the book and I needed to stay on course, and too many opinions can muddy one's thinking; selfish, because it put upon those chosen the horrific task of reading and reading and then, incredibly, reading again, every page of the manuscript until this obsessive writer got it right, or almost right. Once it was accepted for publication, the actual editor had her say.

So to Dorothy Greenberg, whose feisty criticisms kept me clear and honest and whose friendship I could not survive without, I owe a debt of gratitude that I can never repay. (DG: Please note that I said I couldn't, so don't try to extract it!) To Bob Diforio, my agent, who stuck with me and my foot-stomping reactions as well as with the project itself for two years plus, a big thank-you! Thank you also to Colleen Kapklein, my editor, whose fresh eye and black pencil showed me that even when you think you've gone as far as you can go, there's always more that can be done. And to my incredible friends who put up with me in my funks, who never wavered in their conviction that it would get done—and published!—and then withheld their "I told you so"s: I love you all.

To my mentor, Susanne Schad-Somers, who put a foot in my back and kept pushing: No amount of thank-yous will ever be enough. You opened up doors I hadn't known existed and generously invited me to walk through. The only thing that I can give back is the promise that I will pass it all on.

Finally, to my clients whose stories I have used (albeit camouflaged) and to those I haven't, a secret: All those times you thought you were learning from me, I was also learning from you. Without your willingness to learn, sometimes only in increments, sometimes with flying leaps of faith, I would never have been able to develop the techniques and concepts found in these pages. I am forever grateful.

CONTENTS

SAY IT

WITH

confidence

INTRODUCTION

I picked up the phone. The woman's words came rushing at me as if a pause would allow her to change her mind. "My company wants me giving presentations. I hate them. I get so nervous, I get sick at the thought of them. Someone said I should try pills, but I don't want to take pills. I've taken other presentation skills courses, but they didn't help. A friend said you could. Can you?" After I managed to get her name, I probed for more information. In my line of work you have to move slowly and listen carefully, because the reasons people have trouble with speaking in public can range from a lack of understanding of the skill itself, all the way to a deep-seated phobia. I assumed that she probably was not a true phobic, because phobics rarely put themselves into situations that could involve confronting their fears. Still, as the last thing I ever want to do is open up a can of worms that

I cannot contain, I asked what had occurred in the other courses. She answered that they hadn't related to the types of presentations she made. "Listen!" she said. "What I really want to know is, can you help me develop a unique, strong presentation style so that when I stand up and present, people will listen?" I explained that the idea wasn't to develop a separate style for presentations, but to enhance the way she presents herself daily. "Splitting styles is like splitting personalities," I said. "It's terribly disconcerting to both you and your audience. It also means that you've left part of yourself somewhere else." "Oh!" she said in a voice that seemed to disappear into her thoughts. "Is that why I feel so alone when I present?" The process had begun. We had exposed the first of whatever misconceptions she had about presenting, misconceptions that inhibited her from being in control of herself, her material, and her audience. We all have such misconceptions—misconceptions that not only inhibit us from being effective presenters, but also may keep us from attempting to learn *how* to present effectively. This book exposes the ten most common misconceptions. However, there are two others that, while I haven't allotted them their own chapters, run through the book like recurring themes and therefore need to be highlighted here.

The first misconception is that we only "present" when we are in front of an "audience"—the definition of *audience* in this case being the first definition found in most dictionaries, that is, a group of spectators at a public event. This is what my caller believed. This is what is accepted by most people. Yet, the reality is that *we all make presentations every day—all day.*

Whether we express an idea at a meeting, sell a product or service, have a discussion with our spouse over finances, ask our boss for a raise, converse with friends about politics, or try to inveigle the butcher into slicing us that special cut of meat—we are presenting. It makes no difference whether we do so to one person we know, a thousand we don't, or vice versa—*a presentation is a presentation is a presentation*—of our wants, needs, ideas, and, most important, of our self. I do not wish to imply that the presenter is the most important part of a presentation, although it happens that if an audience accepts the presenter it may also accept the presenter's content. However, to get back to the butcher, the quality of your food is apt to hinge not on how important your dinner's success is to you, but on whether you can make its success matter to the person behind the counter. As we shall see, the way to make something important to someone else is to focus on that person and his or her needs—to relate what you yourself want to something he or she wants, and somehow to connect the two—to step outside yourself, so to speak. That's no easy feat when how we present ourselves and our ideas is intertwined with our sense of who we are and how we see our self, that is, our persona—our self-image—but, as we shall also see, it can be done.

The second misconception has to do with our attitude toward those whom we view as appearing to enjoy the opportunity to address an audience. We think of them as rare birds, people with a message, performers! Often we assume they were born with special talents. Sometimes we label them exhibitionists, egocentric personalities, "show-offs." We may even go so far as to say that those who enjoy speaking in public must be slightly out of their minds. The concept that we, too, might possess the same impulses that go into creating a performer either does not enter our mind, or if it does, we see these impulses as something negative, unseemly, not quite proper. Here too, as in the previous misconception, reality, and perception differ. *We are all latent performers*. Now, before you react with "Not I!" let me clarify that statement. We are all latent performers in that we all want to be seen, heard, and applauded. Or, put another way, all of us want validation, acceptance, and approval. What we don't want is to make fools of ourselves. It is that fear of making fools of ourselves that distorts our impulse to go for—in a straightforward, unabashed manner—the very validation, acceptance, and approval that we want. This fear did not always exist. When we are very young, we not only *want* to be seen, heard, and applauded, we *need* to be seen, heard, and applauded. Watch a toddler show off his or her belly button and you'll see this wondrous exhibitionism in its purest form, an exhibitionism that is a normal stage in our development—between two and three years of age—when we need to prance and strut our stuff for doting, adoring parents. We need to do that so we can develop a strong enough sense of self to then allow us to leave this period and go on to the next developmental stage, in which validation of skills becomes more important than validation of existence. Still, life "ain't" perfect. Not all parents dote and adore. Not all parents are capable of responding as we need them to respond, and, for the vast majority of us, events usually do occur that can produce conflicting attitudes toward "performing." For example, when one of my clients was a young boy he was transferred to a new school, where he found himself to be a good year ahead of his class. He was an extremely bright but, admittedly, hyperactive child, and the combination of his own hyperactivity, along with the understandable boredom he experienced, eventually overcame him. At a particular point, he became so frustrated that when another child did not have the answer to the teacher's question, my client remembers jumping up and shouting it out for him. "*E, e, e,* it's the letter *EEEEE*!" he yelled at the top of his voice. The teacher, who, to make matters worse, just happened to be my client's favorite, sent him to the corner and made him stay there for the rest of the day. Granted, she was punishing him for his behavior, but he felt as if he was being punished for knowing the correct answer. There were probably many more incidents such as this, but this is the one my client remembers, the one that shamed him into "learning" his lesson. He learned it so well that eventually he found it nearly impossible to speak up at meetings, voice his ideas with clients, and interact with others. As we said, life isn't perfect. If it were, we would all emerge from childhood without a mark on us. Instead, most of us "learn" that what should be pleasurable and natural can quickly turn into something intertwined with shame and dread. Of course, in a world where "pride goeth before destruction," it would be unrealistic to expect that most parents and teachers would not do whatever was needed to make certain that our pride did not turn into that "haughty spirit which goeth before a fall" (Proverbs 16:18).

Misconceptions: the hidden enemy. It is not what we don't know, but what we think we do know that can present the biggest obstacle to developing our self and abilities. For instance, you may believe that by the time you reach adulthood, you should be able to present yourself and your ideas with panache, and if you can't, then there must be something wrong with you. That's a reasonable assumption, since the way we present ourselves is a conglomeration of all that we were taught, directly or through example, by parents, teachers, peers, and those we consciously and unconsciously chose as role models. Yet I'd wager that few of us had a father like that of one woman I knew, who, after he'd taken a course in public speaking, demanded that his children stand and either tell a story or relate their day's events every night after dinner. Whatever negative ramifications these required performances had on the children—and there were a few—to this day they are all able to stand in front of an audience of any size and speak concisely and effectively. More than likely the majority of us were admonished that "silence is golden" and "children should be seen and not heard"—two not particularly helpful lessons in the development of strong, concise speaking skills.

The accepted definition of *misconception* is that it is an erroneous notion, a mistaken thought. I must add to that one more: a virus. Thoughts do not live in a vacuum. Just as one single idea can infect—to the good or ill—ours and others' thoughts and deeds, a misconception can distort aspect after aspect of our behavior, affecting everything with which it comes into contact. For instance, the "reasonable" assumption that "by now you should be able to present well" could cause you to approach presentation skills training with the mind-set of a Doubting Thomas. At the first encountered difficulty, you well might assume that you lack the facility and give up—if, that is, you approach training at all. You could even spend your life avoiding situations in which you'd be required to present, which, in this highly competitive society, limits career growth.

How misconceptions form. Ideas get passed from generation to generation without a check of their validity. In part this occurs because of the authoritative manner in which most information gets passed down to us from parents and teachers, until even the most rebellious among us eventually accepts "because I said so" as proof positive. It also occurs because, as children, we tend to accept as valid whatever we're told by authority figures, because remaining on good terms with those who have a direct effect on our everyday lives is a major component of surviving childhood relatively intact. It's no wonder that if we were told as children that we were introverted or extroverted, or too assertive or not assertive enough, that we will have a difficult time accepting that this may not actually be the case, or believing that it's possible for us to change.

The earlier in our lives an idea gets planted, the more firmly rooted it becomes. This is why we often accept—lock, stock, and barrel—ideas that, if we stopped and thought about them, would make no sense. For instance, no one could argue rationally that any of us popped out of the womb able to speak with a resonant voice, enunciate clearly, and make dramatic use of our facial expressions, all while remaining totally in control of our other body parts. No matter. The belief still persists that certain people are simply "born presenters," and it persists with a vengeance. When I tried to get one client past her commitment to the idea of the "born presenter," she countered that her sister, with whom she was quite competitive, "just got people to ooh and aah even when she was six months old!" I had no easy task convincing her that people love to "ooh" and "aah" at babies simply because they are babies and not because of any conscious effort or ability to enthrall on the babies' part— her sister included. She continued to cling to her belief even as I suggested that her parents might well have reinforced the myth until all in the family accepted as gospel the sister's innate talents, and that then those "talents" were nurtured until the myth became a reality.

Before you argue nurture versus nature theories, I do not dispute the part genetics play in how we present ourselves. They define our limitations and program our biological clocks. However, they cannot tell us what those limitations are or how we will actually behave. Even if all goes according to plan, both biologically and environmentally, so that, for instance, we walk and talk at the appointed times, how well and in what manner we will do so will have less to do with our genes than with other forces within and without ourselves. Raised by wolves, we will probably stay on all fours; brought up in a home where "dese, dems, and dose" are the norm, we will speak in "dem" terms, no matter how much blue blood may be coursing through our veins. Put another way, you will speak the language of the country where you were born, as well as, or instead of, the language your birth parents speak.

We come to our ideas, beliefs, and attitudes by processing information based not only on what we were taught—both formally and informally—but also on our own powers of observation. However, all that we hear, see, or read does not reach us without being filtered through whatever knowledge we have already acquired, our own preconceived ideas, our mood of the moment, and, yes, even our desires. We observe the exact same beggar on the street day after day. Whether we see the beggar as a charlatan one morning or as someone in need on another day could depend on whether or not we, ourselves, are feeling particularly needy or if, the night before, we watched a thought-provoking piece on homelessness on the tube that made us resolve to do more. In other words: same beggar, same observer, yet two very different observations. This accounts for why one day we may dig into our pocket and on another we might walk by totally immune to the outstretched hand. In another scenario, we are invited to a dance concert. Our friend, a dancer herself, knows the piece intimately. We arrive late and miss the announcement that an understudy will play the lead. Our friend sees the understudy enter, take off in the wrong direction, and throw all the other dancers into disarray, while we see a rather bizarre piece of choreography. What we know, or think we know, changes the information we take in as well as our conclusions. Then there are times that we see only what we want to see. We miss signals of insecurity in someone we wish were secure, signals of hostility in someone we wish were kind, signals of self-centeredness in someone we wish were giving. We are even capable of turning a homely person into someone quite beautiful by simply focusing on one attractive feature and disregarding whatever is not appealing.

To validate each piece of information we take in, we would have to treat every aspect of our life as a scientific experiment. Even then, we may not have access to or know about information that could validate our assumptions; or our need to be proven right may outweigh any desire to seek the truth; or that truth may so threaten our equilibrium, we'd rather avoid it altogether. If we discover one of our ideas to be "off," what others may also be? And if we've held these beliefs for a long time and invested considerable energy in them, built our lives on them, then what? Will we have to remake our entire lives? Can we?

To uncover and root out a misconception takes a strong will, a bit of work, and plenty of luck. Keep in mind that what we accept as fact we rarely feel compelled to discuss; and whatever we do not discuss cannot be refuted. Because we tend to gravitate toward like-minded individuals, opportunities to hear opposing ideas can be infrequent. Even if we're with those who may disagree with us, they may not feel free to say so, as a great many of us prefer to avoid confrontation. Who has not been in a situation where we've bitten our tongue rather than provoke dissension? Something or someone must put our ideas to the test—something such as a slip of the tongue, an innocent remark, or an action that provokes us to react. As if all this isn't enough, someone must be around to challenge us; someone who we believe may know something that we don't. Until this occurs we have no way of affirming whether or not our ideas are on target or ill conceived. All this is my way of saying that we should not feel lacking because we harbor various misconceptions, as long as we're open to scrutinizing our ideas when the opportunity arises, and we certainly should not feel bad if we are filled with misconceptions about presentation of self and ideas. Misconceptions on this subject could—and, as you will see, do—fill a book.

Don't for a minute believe that levels of expertise, salary, and position protect us against fallacious thinking. I've found many of the same misconceptions held by CEOs and entry-level staffers. As an example, one business owner told me—in no uncertain terms—that he looked upon his employees as his friends, and he was quite certain that they regarded him in the same way. Although I tried, there was no arguing with him. How do you reprimand a friend? I asked. Promote one "friend" over another? Worse, how do you fire "friends"? Obviously, you don't! Not without risking the loss of a friendship. He so needed to believe that he was loved, however, that he clung to his belief, which has caused him to make a number of poor management decisions that have hurt his company. The irony is that the only people who could actually make him see the light (that is, his employees) would be crazy to do so.

Misconceptions are not confined to any one area of thought. We all hold a variety of cultural, political, sociological, and psychological misconceptions. However, because my field is that of communication and presentation, this book deals with misconceptions about how we present ourselves and our ideas. It is my intent to expose and contradict as many misconceptions as possible so that you the reader, whether you are someone who would prefer jumping into a snake pit to standing up and speaking in public, or someone who simply wants to improve the way you present, can move past where you are and become a truly effective presenter. We will look at misconceptions about what you may think you're expressing by an action and what you are actually communicating; about what you may presume to be at the root of another's behavior and how those assumptions may cause you to react in particular ways; about natural versus acquired talents and your ability or inability to change; and about training, rehearsing, and preparation in general. (You may be surprised to learn what some people consider to be adequate preparation and what actually is.) It is incredible the myriad of inhibitors we carry about!

Keep in mind that you do not need to be a mesmerizing, dynamic presenter in order to be effective. Variety *is* the spice of life for an audience. If all public speakers spoke like Mario Cuomo, the former governor of New York, who brought down the house at the Democratic Convention of 1988 and again in

1992, we would rapidly become bored. As a matter of fact, it is possible that one of the reasons Cuomo lost to Pataki in 1994 is that voters became so used to his style of oration, they stopped listening. Familiarity with style often ends up causing us to relish "the show" rather than paying close attention to the content. Although politicians are usually the first people who come to mind when we think about effective presenters, we all have encountered others: the teacher who enticed us to delve into a subject we never thought interesting, the salesperson who got us to buy an item we weren't sure of, the person who at the last community meeting was able calmly to express a minority view without being shouted down.

As we shall see, effective communication occurs when nothing interferes with the transmission of information between speaker and audience—neither physical barriers such as disconcerting mannerisms, which can estrange an audience from the speaker, nor mental barriers such as disconcerting thoughts, which can estrange the speaker from himself. To be an effective presenter you will need to develop the skills that will enable you to focus on your audience, to share with your audience.

Effective presenters always appear to want to share their passion with their audience. I say "appear," because not all who have the ability to hold us spellbound care about us or our well-being. They do, however, appear to be concerned, and it is that appearance that draws us to them. On the flip side, ineffective presenters not only appear, but usually are, totally involved with themselves. They worry about how well they're doing, what we think about them, whether we like them or—heaven forbid!—do not. We, the audience, function solely as their mirror, assuming, that is, we exist for them at all.

The uncovering of a misconception, even admitting to ourselves that we have one, is only the first step to dismantling it. Next you need to incorporate into your daily life your new patterns of thinking. This does not happen overnight. Old thoughts, even erroneous ones, die hard, as do physical habits. If you have slumped for years, it takes more than one visit to a physical therapist to correct your posture. In order for you to reach whatever goals you decide to set for yourself, you must tackle both the mental and physical aspects of presenting simultaneously. This is why, along with the dismantling of each misconception about speaking in public (and for that matter, private), I have included exercises that will help you to develop your physical skills. I beg that you try each one as it arises. Not to do so would be like attempting to learn the art of cooking from a cookbook without ever entering a kitchen.

However, do not continue to practice everything at once. The best way to approach the different exercises you will find dispersed throughout this book is to practice each skill separately until you feel you're beginning to master its particular techniques. Then, move on to another. For those aspects of self you wish to change that do not necessarily involve other people, work alone and/or with an instructor. For those aspects that do involve other people, begin by practicing alone, but then repeat the process with others present. If you continue to practice on a regular basis, eventually the skills will meld together and become an integral part of yourself.

Every skill you integrate into your normal way of doing things is one less you need to think about when you are in front of an audience.

This is a process that takes time. I would like to tell you that by reading this book you'll be able to fast forward to giving extraordinary performances. I can't. First, I don't know what skills you already possess, what goals you wish to set for yourself, or how much effort you are willing to expend to reach those goals. What I can promise you is that by reading on, you will develop insights about your presentation of self, and that as you incorporate the exercises into your daily routine, the walls that have inhibited your interaction with others will begin to crumble. To those of you with whom I've been fortunate enough to work: Use this book to remind you of the areas we covered (or uncovered, as the case may be) as well as to discover others not touched upon. To all others: If this book succeeds in dispelling only one misconception which has been holding you back, then it will have been well worth the effort.

CHAPTER 1

Misconception: "I can't—not me."

Here's a fascinating paradox—one that never ceases to amaze me. Many of the people who attend workshops to improve the way they communicate are the very same people who, when asked to do something that will help them improve the way they communicate, dig their heels into the status quo and state adamantly, "I can't do that. It's just not me." This is an incredible reaction, as these people must know that to become more effective in the way they present requires that they will have to alter some aspect of their thinking, behavior, or demeanor. According to my quite worn *Random House Unabridged Dictionary,* to *improve* "usually implies a remedying of a felt or perceived lack or need," and there's no way we can "remedy" the way we present ourselves, without emending our style of presentation. Do these recalcitrant clients believe they are doomed, like leopards, to retain their particular

17

spots forever? Unlikely. Their decision to attend a workshop acknowledges a desire on their part for change, or they wouldn't have signed up. While it is true that some people come secretly wishing for a magic wand, a sleight of hand that can right their world, turning them overnight into a magnetic personality, the vast majority come to learn and to grow. Yet over and over again, I hear that same protestation: "I can't! It's just not me."

I have no doubt that all of us, at one time or another, have reacted to a suggested change in this fashion. One might even argue that because it is such a common reaction, it has validity—majority rule and all that. Yet the idea that we cannot attempt something different because it is "not me" makes the assumption that there exists a "me" so precious, so carved in stone, that it cannot be touched without incurring harm. This idea is, without a doubt, one of the most inhibiting of the misconceptions regarding presentation of both self and materials. This is the reason I have chosen to tackle it first. Unless we understand what lies at the root of this misconception, we will not be able to get on with the process of learning how to present our self and our ideas effectively. Therefore, I will start by breaking the misconception into its two parts: the "I can't" and the "It's not me."

Part I: "I Can't"

Fear not! I won't raise the "can't means won't" issue. We all know that there are some things we simply

can't do. We can't leap from the thirtieth floor
without a parachute and live; nor can we survive
underwater for an hour without oxygen. Also, contrary
to current teaching, we cannot be anything we want to
be. Without an incredibly formed larynx, superb vocal
cords, large sinus cavities for resonance, vast amounts
of stamina, as well as an ear for music and a mathe-
matical mind (there appears to be a strong correlation
between math and musical prowess) we cannot
become a Pavarotti. Just as all the flour, sugar, milk,
baking powder, shortening, eggs, and vanilla extract
in the world will not produce a chocolate cake without
chocolate, we can only go as far as our staples will
allow. We can, however, be more than we are. While
we may be limited by our biological heritage, the
parameters of those limitations are unknown. Like the
runner who breaks all records and then finds the inner
strength to break one more, we have no real idea of our
actual capabilities. We humans can be so amazing, so
resilient, so surprising that even those who have been
labeled "with limited capacity" have often gone on to
surpass the experts' expectations. We need only
remind ourselves of the physically disabled and
learning-impaired children who compete in the
Special Olympics—children who not so very long ago
would have been left to rot in barbaric institutions—
to understand how none of us knows exactly of what
we are capable.

As there's no denying that growth requires change,
why do so many people who know that change must
be part of the process of learning apply the brakes—
and with such force?

Change Threatens

If we look at change in the broadest sense, it entails encountering something new, something that is unfamiliar. In other words, change, by its very nature, provokes feelings of loss of control. Ernest Becker, in his Pulitzer Prize–winning treatise, *The Denial of Death,* states that change implies risk, that risk leads to the unknown, and, as there is no greater unknown than death, change can be an oppressive reminder of our mortality. This theory makes perfect sense when we look at how we humans, who certainly have the capacity to change our behavior, act compared to other creatures who do not have the capacity to change. Take, for instance, the spider. Ingeniously designed to be capable of picking prime locations to entrap her prey, a spider cannot change careers after a debilitating battle with a web-destroying broom. Sweep away the web, and the spider will begin spinning all over again. It has no choice. We, on the other hand, do. When the metaphoric broom sweeps at us, we have the ability to decide whether it should be business as usual or change the way we go about our affairs. Yet, while we may promise ourselves to diet after a heart-stopping attack of indigestion or to drive more defensively after narrowly missing another car, we usually return to hot fudge sundaes and passing in the fast lane. Becker's thesis states that we return to our customary behavior not because nature programmed us thus, or because we wish to die, but in order for us to pretend that death does not wait for us, to defy it. It is difficult enough to live life as it is; it is nearly impossible to strive toward a better future with the inevitability of our demise hovering overhead. If our subconscious equates change with dying, no wonder we find change so threatening.

My father loved to tell about an eighty-year-old man who, pardoned by the governor after having served sixty years of a life term, was back, after only three days of freedom, banging at the governor's gates, begging to be returned to prison. When the astounded governor asked the man why he would want to give up his freedom, a new home, the sun! to go back to a cold cell with filthy walls, leaking faucets, terrible smells, and roaches, the old man replied, "Ah, but they are *my* filthy walls, *my* leaking faucets, *my* terrible smells—*MY* roaches." We all carry within us aspects of the old man. Many of us will live with incredible discomfort rather than alter the status quo. Some, who suffer from loneliness, will opt to remain alone rather than confront their fears of meeting new people; others stay in difficult or even abusive relationships rather than risk the unknown; and still others stay in unrewarding jobs rather than face the fears that prevent them from moving on.

Take the story of a man whom I will call Norman. A most personable man in his late thirties, Norman works in the neighborhood hardware store. One day he mentioned that he had turned down a chance to run for his community's school board. When I asked why, he told me that the thought of speaking in public made him ill. I suggested that he get help, that the fear can be relatively easy to overcome. He refused, saying that he really had no need of the school board,

and anyway, getting up in public just wasn't "him"—
that "Can't. Not me" refrain again.

One assumes that a person's resistance to change
would be in direct proportion to the risk the change
involves, yet the changes I ask clients to make are
usually slight. What risk exists in standing up
straighter, controlling the use of one's hands, learning
how to modulate a voice? If my clients know that the
status quo can be improved simply by their
enhancing the way they interact with others, why
should any of these enhancements produce inhibiting
anxiety? Simply stated, change exposes our inadequacies. Put another way, if it needs fixing, something isn't working. Not an easy thing to admit.
Often, painful.

Change and the Fear of Shame

In the past, most people, if asked what they were
afraid of about speaking in public, used to answer
"Making a fool of myself." Nowadays, most reply
"Fear of failure." It has become a catchall phrase, yet
the old response is much closer to the truth. It is the
fear of being made to appear a fool—the fear of
shame—that stops most of us from attempting
change. We can look like idiots as we attempt change,
and we can expose our inadequacies when we admit to
needing to change. I believe it is this fear that lay at
the root of Norman's response—not the fear of
shaming himself as he learned to speak in public, but
the shame of what could occur once he did. Norman

often joked about his lack of social skills. Imagine his
dread of finding himself in unfamiliar situations,
having to interact with people from diverse back-
grounds, people whose social skills he imagined to be
better than his own. That certainly would explain his
"no thanks" to the first step that could put him on the
school board, which would then place him in a situation in which he could shame himself—or so he
thought—on a regular basis.

Carl Goldberg, in *Understanding Shame,* emphatically states that "shame is the most complex and least
understood emotion that the human race has yet
evolved." Whether we wish to go that far, there's no
denying that the fear of being shamed in front of
another person can be one of life's great inhibitors—
whether that person be a stranger, teacher, peer, family
member, or simply ourselves. One woman I know,
who had always been a poor test taker in school,
admitted that years ago, when a newspaper article
showed examples of high school exam questions, she
couldn't bring herself to attempt to answer them even
in the privacy of her home. The chance that she might
not get the answers right, even though no one would
ever know, inhibited her from trying. It wasn't the
failure she feared, but the shame the failure could
induce.

According to the *Oxford English Dictionary,* the lin-
guistic roots of *shame* may lie in a pre-Teutonic word
meaning "to cover oneself," that is, "to hide." Even
today the German word *scham* translates, according to
Langenscheidt's German-English Dictionary as "1) shame
2) bashfulness and anat. 3) genitals." Whether we

wish to "fall through the floor," "disappear," "get the hell out and never go back," the discomfort associated with shame can be overwhelming. Even thinking about the time we broke our aunt's favorite dish or burst loudly into a room where a closed-door meeting was in process or blurted out something we shouldn't have, can cause the color to rush to our face, beads of perspiration to form, a queasiness in the stomach, or whatever particular personal symptoms—physical or emotional—we experience when we are overwhelmed with shame. Interestingly, these are the very same symptoms induced by stage fright.

Years ago, on *The Tonight Show,* Johnny Carson tried to cajole the actress Patricia Neal to reveal what had allowed her to play a particularly emotional and debasing scene in the film *Days of Wine and Roses.* Looking like a highly remorseful Lizzie Borden, she mumbled that she had thought about something awful she had done as a child. Carson, his curiosity fueled, kept at her, until, finally, she tearfully blurted out that she had thrown a half grapefruit at her best friend when she was four years old. Everyone, including Carson, giggled until they realized the depth of her pain. Carson tried to convince her that a childish pique was nothing to be embarrassed about, but we could all see that the shame—which most likely had stemmed from a severe adult admonishment rather than from the deed itself—was not going away so easily.

Shame induces rage. If you've ever felt like throwing something after you've been called on the carpet—even for something you indeed may have done—you have experienced the rage that shame can bring. Some people turn that rage inward against themselves—producing depression. Others vent their rage: a slam of the door; a fist pounding a desk; music turned up real loud. Shame provokes rage. Rage is loss of control, and loss of control publicly displayed produces shame. Think of the expression "I lost it" and the embarrassment losing it brings. There are many ways in which we can feel we've lost it. For instance, because we achieve proficiency at any skill by repetition, as we attempt to acquire a skill, we go through a period of not only insecurity, but awkwardness. As we learn we risk exposing ourselves to the possibility of being shamed, that is, to ridicule, which in turn might provoke us to rage and even more shame. If we are made to feel like an idiot in the attempt, the shame can be devastating. One person at a workshop, an ex-actress, never forgave me for asking her to do a particular speech exercise along with the rest of the group. She had wanted to show off her skills and told me later that she was horrified that I would "shame" her (her word) by asking her to perform an exercise rather than allowing her to perform for the others.

Retrospective shame. Then there is the moment when we realize that what we have been doing all along could have been done not only differently, but better. As we recall those earlier incidents, each remembrance becomes its own shaming moment, and all those moments accumulate. For instance, we may not have known that when we talk in front of a group we weave back and forth—a common symptom of nervousness. At the moment we become aware of our behavior, we may start to remember other presentations when we weaved—presentations in front of people who, we now realize, could have thought that we were slightly inebriated. Give us enough bad memories and we begin to experience retrospective shame, and accumulated shame can feel overwhelming.

Another example: Imagine that you are the son of a mother who loves poetry and a father, an English professor, whose dreams of writing the great American novel never materialized and who projected his lost dreams onto you. From an early age you realize that if you make words rhyme, your father will call you his "Amadeus of poetry." You have no idea what it means, except that you can hear the approval in his voice and see his eyes light up—quite different from those times when you don't feel like reciting, and he treats you as if you don't exist, and your mother gives you looks of disapproval. So you rhyme away anytime he asks as well as for anyone else who will listen, convinced that this is the one thing that makes you "special" and the only way to everyone's heart. Then, on the night before your eighth birthday, after you have written a new poem that you plan to recite at your party, you overhear an aunt say to your mother, "Let me tell you, Ellen, if you don't stop James from making us listen to little Jimmy reciting that drivel, we're going to stop coming." The young man who told me this story described it as the most horrific moment of his life. He was devastated to realize that every time he had "showed off" his "talents" in the past he had not only been not appreciated, but he had been seen as ridiculous. His rhymes were not great poetry, but recitations to be endured. Worse yet, he had been misled by those he had trusted most—his parents. He developed incredible inner conflicts about writing or speaking anything that he had composed. Eventually all forms of oral communication became involved in this conflict. He could no longer trust himself to evaluate his own ability to write or speak well, but this did not stop him from wanting to write or speak. The need to gain his father's approval remained, but now, the need was associated with a shaming experience. This is not to say that the young man's parents shouldn't have encouraged him to write, but they should have done this so that he could acquire pride in his own accomplishments, and not as a way to win their love.

As I stated in the introduction, it is appropriate for a toddler to be exhibitionistic. It is not only appropriate, but healthy, mandatory, for emotional growth. It is also necessary that during that period a parent applaud the child's exhibitionism. What is not appropriate is for the parent to encourage or even demand that the behavior go on past the appropriate age. If this is done, the exhibitionistic phase continues, eventually taking on a life of its own, which is why the young man found himself unconsciously dealing with two opposing impulses: 1) to win his father's approval, and 2) never to be shamed again. He compromised by continuing to write, but badly. He even managed to flunk English so that his father would have to provide him with tutors.

Change Can Mean Loss

A third reason we may resist change has to do with giving up what psychologists term *secondary gains,* defined as the "benefits derived from being disabled" or the benefits (attention) derived from acting in a self-destructive fashion (from *Abnormal Psychology and Modern Life,* by Robert Carson and James Butcher). Here are examples of this syndrome: 1) Someone whose illnesses are an unconscious way of receiving longed for attention and caretaking. While an illness may start out legitimately enough, people who never received a sufficient amount of "good" attention when they were healthy, but only got attention when ill, can develop recurring bouts of that illness. 2) Someone who gets sick as a means to avoid a feared situation. I am never surprised if about two days before a workshop a participant calls to "warn" me that he or she is not feeling particularly well, and may be unable to attend. When I explain that there are no refunds, that the company has to pay or send an alternate, they somehow manage to get over whatever they felt "coming on." 3) Someone who continually fails so as not to compete with an authority figure. 4) Someone who makes self-deprecating remarks in order to receive compliments. We have all met this type and, I would dare say, have even once or twice used this technique ourselves. Finally, 5) a person who provokes others to anger in the mistaken belief that even negative attention is preferable to no attention at all.

Aleah. A quite extreme example of this last behavior is Aleah. As you read on, you shouldn't be surprised that she was able to attain and maintain employment. Her job was to read manuscripts, a task that does not require great social interaction.

Aleah believed herself to be the victim of everyone's hostile behavior. She regaled her psychotherapist with story after story about co-workers maltreating her, grimacing, pouting, making faces as she did so. Friends were almost nonexistent. Her therapist, aware that Aleah's physical mannerisms could provoke Mother Teresa to rage, suggested that Aleah attend a communication skills workshop. As the therapist explained, he could not and would not take on the task of modifying her antisocial behavioral mannerisms because doing so could damage the patient/therapist relationship. A patient coming to terms with an abusively critical parent would be justified in confusing the therapist with the parent if the therapist were continually pointing out and correcting the patient's behavior, which certainly is an unpleasant but necessary component of communication skills training.

Aleah, hell-bent on proving her "innocence," agreed to attend the workshop and even told the therapist to feel free to discuss her case with me. I was not surprised to be warned that Aleah took pleasure in the rejection her actions provoked. According to psychologist Susanne Schad-Somers (*Sadomasochism: Etiology and Treatment*), most childhood victims cling to the victim role long after they themselves have turned into the victimizers. Aleah's doctor told me to "tread carefully!" Just how carefully I would have to tread, I could never have imagined.

Reluctant attendees usually express their qualms in

a phone call or soon after entering the studio. Aleah preferred to behave outrageously. An unusually tall, big-boned woman, she slouched her way over to a seat and, making certain all could see her, screwed up her face to show her anger. Her behavior was that of a morose, petulant six-year-old, not a woman in her late thirties. Much like a child who shuts her eyes, shakes her head violently, and makes loud noises so as not to hear what is being said, Aleah closed herself off from everyone and continued to act out all day.

The other four participants, although not particularly high-powered, were open and friendly and soon found a way to let Aleah know that her attitude made them highly uncomfortable. Still, it wasn't enough for Aleah to display her anger toward me. She was intent on turning the others against me as well. Over lunch, as was relayed to me later by another participant, she labeled me demeaning, harsh, and hurtful.

I decided, due to a combination of 1) the therapist's warning, 2) my understandable concern that Aleah's behavior could negatively affect the others, and 3) my strong aversion to rewarding bad behavior, neither to focus on nor to ignore Aleah— either of which would have placed her exactly where she longed to be: center stage. While I readily admit to teasing clients who need to approach the process with a little more lightness of being, with Aleah, I walked on eggshells.

As I said, communication skills trainers continually need to point out to clients their undesirable habits or behavior, preferably at the very moment they occur. The reason: We cannot eliminate a habit if we can't catch ourselves in the act. Even so, whatever criticism I gave Aleah was done in a most general fashion. Her posture was addressed along with everyone's during the posture exercises and her facial expressions during a group discussion on how we respond to what we see in others. This did not stop her from sniping that I sounded just like a mother. When I did compliment her for the few seconds she stood straight and delighted in her one and only smile, she returned instantly to the slouching, surly child—the secondary gains issues. Children, besides needing positive reinforcement, require age-appropriate attention. If they do not get it, they will go to any extreme to get whatever attention may be available, no matter how negative it may be. While I have no direct knowledge of exactly what transpired to cause Aleah's extreme behavior, it is not difficult to write a scenario of an overly critical mother who found nothing about her child pleasing and a child who developed into a truly unlovable child because of her mother's attitude. Although her mother may have preferred that Aleah disappear into the woodwork, for Aleah to do so would have negated Aleah's very existence, thus placing her in a most untenable situation. If she was good, she would cease to exist in her mother's eye; when she was bad, she forced her mother to "see" her. Again, all children not only desire but need their mother's love and approval in order to flourish. Aleah, like so many psychologically or physically abused children, had to know instinctively that such love could never be attained no matter what she did—a knowledge that can be far more devastating to the emerging child than any reprimand. It was far safer for Aleah to keep hope alive with the fantasy that if she ever decided to be good, she'd receive that love, than to live with the knowledge that no matter what she did, she would not receive her mother's love. (This is the reason so many parentally abused children protect and defend their abusers.) The behavior became ingrained. She did not act out just with her mother but, because nothing entered her life to break the cycle, she continued to act out with everyone around her.

Aleah's inner workings was her therapist's job; mine was to make her aware of the impact her external behavior was having on others. It wasn't easy. Changing meant that she would be giving into her mother's critical demands. Convinced that I was out to shame her any way I could—in her book, a compliment was a criticism, as it pointed up prior bad behavior—I was to be damned for trying, and she would be damned to remain the same.

Still, neither fear of death, fear of shame, nor the potential for secondary gains explains why some people can change certain aspects of themselves and not others. Think of how many people you know who diet to change their weight, exercise or go to plastic surgeons to change their shape, and have no problem demanding that their hair stylist find them a new "me" on a regular basis. Even Norman grows a mustache, shaves it off, and then grows it again on a regular basis. Yet often these are the very people who recoil at the mere suggestion that they change their attitudes or behavior. By the same token, others you know may spend years—not to mention vast amounts of money—working on their internal self through psychotherapy or the like, and at the same time refuse to make an external change of any kind. Stand up straighter? Doesn't feel natural. Change my voice? No way; born with this one. Smile with my eyes? Forget it. I am what I am what I am! Oh, how often I've wanted to shriek, "You're not Popeye, for heaven's sake. You're a real live human being who can change!"

Part II: "It's Not Me"

I often ask clients to define what they see as their particular "me." The responses range from "shy" to "oh, more conservative than *that*" to "well, not so open" to "hey, you know, different." Certainly not descriptions of a "me" carved in stone. Curious, I began to compare those clients who take acquiring a new skill as a challenge or an interesting journey that could lead to positive change, to those who see change as a threat to their being. I soon realized that the "me" to which so many cling is not a "me" that already exists, but one that may not, or at least one that may not have totally evolved into a secure self. Let me explain.

Science tells us that we are comprised of molecules, which come together to form cells that form tissues that become organs that together form the human organism. Within this organism is housed our genes, genes that influence our lives profoundly. They determine our sex, our eye and hair color; they carry the potential for addiction, depression, mania, allergies, cancer, heart diseases—even talent.

However, although we are destined to be influenced by our genes, genes are not our destiny. A family history of cancer may leave us with a predisposition to the disease, but we may not ever be struck down by it. Occurrences in our life, from repeated stress to contact with varying degrees of carcinogenic substances, are what will or will not activate whatever cancer cells lie dormant.

Obviously, the "me" is not a separate entity floating out in space. By its very nature, it is part and parcel of our organism—as much a part as the heart, brain, and liver. Just as these organs are shaped by our biology, chemistry, parents' parenting, circumstance, fate, what have you, the "me" is shaped as well. As the organism can be, and is, affected by everything from illness, to loving, to world events, so too is the "me."

Shakespeare wrote that "love is not love that alters when it alteration finds." I suggest that the reason we so fiercely defend our personal "me" is that we harbor the unconscious suspicion that if we are altered, love will not find us—not a new love, but a love that was never given, one for which we still, for whatever reason, long. In other words, it is the "me" that did not develop, the "me" that wasn't nurtured, that is the one to which we cling.

As the Skin Horse said to the Velveteen Rabbit, "'Real isn't how you are made . . . it's a thing that happens to you. When a child loves you for a long, long time, not just to play with, but REALLY loves you, then you become Real.'" If we substitute the word *parent* for *child* it becomes: Real isn't how you are made . . . it's a thing that happens to you when a parent loves you for a long, long time, not just to play with, but really loves you. Only then do you become real. My point is that among these three groups: 1) those who, early on, did not get a sufficient dose of what psychiatrists refer to as unconditional love, 2) those who got too much—or the wrong kind, and 3) those who got "it" (as Goldilocks would say) "just right," it will be the "just righters" who, most likely, will develop a strong sense of self and be least afraid of change. (Do not confuse the daredevil with someone who is willing to change. There is a difference between "just righters" and those that defy the gods. The first operate out of a sense of inner strength, the second out of a need to prove that they indeed exist.)

A rather successful woman once complained to me about a relative who blamed his lack of success on the fact that his parents had never loved him. "What rubbish!" the woman said. "He was fed, clothed and housed—quite well, if I do say so—whereas we, we were cold and hungry . . . fleeing Russia—on foot no less—and hiding two years in the forest! Why, until I was four years old my milk came from my mother's breast, my warmth from her body!" She had no awareness that although her parents indeed suffered, she herself had received a nurturing that few of us ever do. Although she had a right to carp about her relative's blaming his parents for where he is today, he probably was deprived of a great deal of nourishment, the emotional kind. Do not misunderstand me; I am not saying that whatever we are is due to the quality of our parents' parenting. As the song says, "Parents are people too," with their own problems and personal histories, each with its own series of causes and effects. Certainly parents cannot be blamed for what they have inadvertently passed on to us biologically. Nor is *blame* the appropriate word. A child born to a depressed parent for whom help was not available cannot blame the parent for not being there for the child, but neither can the child blame itself for the adverse effects the parent's depression may have had. What I am saying is that the more secure we are in our overall sense of self, the more we may be willing to try something new, that is, to make changes in the manner in which we present our self. Which is not to say that those who are not secure cannot change. They certainly can, but they need to recognize that by refusing to change, they are preventing themselves from developing the one thing they lack and presumably want the most: confidence.

Before we go on, I need to clarify some terminology: 1) a sense of self, 2) self-esteem, and 3) confidence. They are not interchangeable! They have quite distinct meanings.

A sense of self. There are books, theses, psychologies, endless discussions between academicians, scientists, and the like all trying to explain what is the "self." For our purposes, a sense of self is an awareness of who we are and that we exist separate from others. We can have a realistic sense of self or a faulty sense of self; we can feel "secure" in our self or "insecure;" no matter. It is how we "sense" our self to be.

Self-esteem. This is one of the most overused and misapplied terms in current usage. It should mean how we rate ourselves, but it rarely is used that way. More often than not it is injected as something to be sought after as crusaders once sought the Holy Grail. Considering that we could rate our self on a scale of one to ten as a three, one wonders why one would seek it. As we shall see in chapter 4, one's self-esteem can be enhanced through acquiring skills we can be proud of as well as through therapy to repair egos damaged early. One cannot go to a self-esteem-building class and walk away with self-esteem that is real.

Confidence. Confidence comes from discovering what you need to do, then learning how to do it, and then doing it often enough so that—you guessed it— you can do it with confidence. True confidence comes from reality, not wishful thinking.

Building a "Me"

In *Listening to Prozac*, Peter D. Kramer cites cases of people whose personalities were altered by Prozac, personalities that, according to Kramer, appeared to have been formed by life experiences rather than biology. Even he admits that these cases are rare. Perhaps one day a pill will be developed that can right all the wrongs done to us, but for now I suggest we stick to repairing the damage ourselves. I do not deny that it is easier to acquire most skills when we are young; still, we can always learn new ways of doing things. It is all in how we approach learning itself. Taken as a positive step, one that brings its own rewards, the process can be expansive; taken as a repudiation of who and what we are, it can be agony. Learning is a tool, one you can add to your personal self-improvement kit.

More important, undoing an old habit and replacing it with a new one does not mean that you should condemn yourself to purgatory for having been doing it wrong up to now. Self-flagellation is first of all, a waste of energy and second, misapplied. Unless you were aware that you were doing something wrong as you were doing it, *wrong* is the wrong word to use to describe past behavior.

There is no shame in learning—only in refusing to grow. Each of us has had advantages and disadvantages, and each of us brings something different to the table. To feel inadequate or ashamed because we have not as yet acquired certain skills devalues those we have. The truth is that our birthright is the luck of the draw. We could have been born to immigrants who could barely speak English or parents who taught English in college, gone to a school where the debating team was as important as the varsity squad or one that never required any form of public speaking, or we could have been raised in a home where social graces were of more import than learning, where we were taught how to use finger bowls but not a library. I do not know anyone who had or has everything.

Building a "me" requires work on the whole self, as our internal and external selves are inextricably linked. There's no way we can work on one aspect of our self without affecting another. Nor will we succeed in making the changes permanent and an integral part of our self if we do not pay attention to both. It would be like asking a building contractor to construct a new facade without taking into consideration the structure to which the facade will be attached.

Edwin. Desperate to make a strong impression in a series of job interviews, Edwin came to me demanding that I change his entire persona overnight. I tried to explain this was not a reasonable request. I have learned over time that one should not try to accomplish in an hour what should take weeks. Better to learn one skill well and then move on to another, than to try to redo everything over at the same time. He wouldn't listen. He wanted an immediate redo. Forget that he had poor eye contact, a rather slovenly appearance, and low physical energy. Married, with a newborn child, he was intent on leaving his present firm and going to a more lucrative position. He put everything he had into reworking the way he walked, sat, looked at people, and even responded to questions. During the brief course of our work, Edwin made a number of remarks that revealed an inner conflict about his father, a father who had failed at each business he tried. I pointed out that even if Edwin got the job, unless he resolved the issues he had with his father—with a therapist or the like—the external changes we made together wouldn't stick. He was having none of it. Although he passed all the interviews with flying colors, at the last moment the firm decided not to hire anyone for the position. I would like to tell you that Edwin continued working on his skills, went into therapy, discovered he did not have to relive his father's life, and went on to bigger and better things. He did not. Sadly, rather than view the process as indicative of just what potential he actually possessed, Edwin simply gave up. I raise this issue so that as you read you remember that a truly effective presentation of self is achieved not by simply learning how to put on a face for company, but by making certain that the "face" becomes an integral part of your personality.

As previously stated, confidence comes from knowing what to do, learning how to do it, and then doing it often enough so that you can do "it" with confidence. In other words, the more skills you have, the more confidence you will have in your capabilities. The more confidence, the more secure you will feel in your ability to risk change. So, here's a "to do": Make a list. Write down what you already do well, whether it be cooking a particular dish, problem solving, crunching numbers, playing golf, working the Internet, playing checkers. If you know how to do it, write it down. This is your "have list." Keep it handy to remind you that you are not without skills. It's a sort of security blanket so that as you attempt new skills, you will not overlook what you already possess.

Now there's no law that says we need to initiate more change than what takes place in the normal course of events. We can remain where we are—just like Norman, the clerk in the hardware store—but what a waste of whatever time we have, never to discover of what we are capable. Besides, as everything changes around us, fighting change sets us up to fail.

Keep in mind that, like it or not, from conception until we die, we change. We are not at birth who we are at five, ten, twenty-five, or seventy-five. Nor would we want to be. As someone quite bright once said, any person who is the same at twenty as at fifty has wasted thirty years. I see no reason why you should waste another minute. Therefore, read on!

CHAPTER 2

Misconception: "It should feel natural."

To date, I can remember only one client who, as he attempted to learn a new technique, said, albeit jokingly, "If it doesn't feel natural, I must be doing something right, right?" Right! To paraphrase Oscar Wilde, appearing natural can be a most difficult pose to keep up. It is far more common for me to hear "This doesn't feel right. I must be doing something wrong" or "This doesn't feel right, it must be wrong for me." These are rather knee-jerk reactions when we consider how long it has taken us to learn whatever other skills we possess. We certainly crawled before we walked. We learned to speak over a period of years, and we add to our vocabulary, both individually and societally, on a regular basis. In the 1994 *Webster's New Universal Unabridged Dictionary,* the only word with *cyber-* as a prefix is *cybernetics,* defined as the "study of human control functions and of mechanical and electric

41

systems designed to replace them, involving the application of statistical mechanics to communication engineering." There's no reference in the definition to computers; no listing in the dictionary for *cyberspace*. And, no matter whether or not we have a proclivity toward sports, we do not expect to pick up a golf club or the like and master the game in a short period of time, yet when it comes to the way in which we present ourselves, if we do not quickly feel at home with a new approach, we assume not only that it may never feel right, but that it is probably not right for us. The operative word here is *for*—for while there is some overlap between the misconception that something should feel natural and the "I Can't. Not me" misconception of chapter 1, there is a difference. "I can't. Not me!" applies the brakes before any attempt at change takes place; that is, it shows a basic resistance to change, whereas with "It should feel natural," the resistance occurs after change has been attempted. This misconception has all to do with our expectations regarding change: how change should feel; how long it should take for the change to set in; and whether or not whatever behavior we now call ours is too ingrained to allow change to take place.

The dictionary defines *natural* as that which exists in or is formed by nature. We can say that with a little help from our parents, we are naturally formed, yet, as newborns, we sometimes need someone else's helping hand to start up one of the most natural acts of all—breathing! With a slap, we start. Without that slap, we may be too stuffed up to get in that first gasp. Not that we end up breathing correctly, most of us do not.

Correct breathing, "natural" breathing, starts from the diaphragm. Yet few of us, after we have learned to crawl, stand and walk, know how to breathe diaphragmatically. This is why in order for opera singers to sing, stage actors to project, orators to orate, they must learn how to breathe all over again. Dancers learn to move on the breath, yogis learn to breathe with their entire body, and athletes are taught specific breathing techniques for their particular sport. Breathing may be natural, but natural breathing is not.

Natural vs. Learned Behavior

Early in the twentieth century learned behavior was not even considered a factor in our developmental process. Rather, inherited traits were believed to be at the root of everything. Mental illness or cancer in a family was kept hidden from public knowledge; the faintest whisper could taint chances of marriage. Looks, talent, mental and physical abilities—or their lack—were traceable to particular family members dead and alive; mothers were checked out to see how daughters would age; fathers as to who the sons would become; ancestral roots for what one's own fate might be. Then, when science couldn't validate the genetic myths, the belief in heredity receded and we went through a period during which our environment— physical, mental, and emotional—took over academic thought. Lack of talent, it was thought, could, and should be countered by training. A child's mental prowess was expandable with constant input. The pendulum had swung, reaching what I consider to be its farthest point when patients were made to feel guilty for not being able to cure themselves of a terminal illness.

Now that molecular biology increasingly can prove what was once only old wives' tales, genetics have again hit the front page. Scientists are locating the genes that predispose people to illness, behavior, even personality traits. They are discovering that we appear to be programmed to enter different stages at appropriate points in time. For instance, one study, cited in Bowlby's *Attachment and Loss,* proves that our ability to suckle is not a reaction to offered food, but a skill we're born with, as babies will suck only on a bottle shaped like a nipple. Sucking or rooting is just one dot on our massive genetic blueprint,which, if all goes well, also determines that we'll sit up without support around the end of the seventh month, take our first step at an average of thirteen to fifteen months, and say "dada" by ten months and "mama" by eleven months. There is even one theory, originating with Noam Chomsky and put forth more recently by Stephen Pinker, that we are born with a neural network in our brain that is wired for grammar. Have we come full circle? No. What we have done is to begin to unravel the extraordinary interplay between genetics and environment. We are finding out not only how the mind influences the body but how the body influences the mind; how some forms of mental illness can be chemically induced and corrected, others helped with the talking cure, that is, psychotherapy and the like, and other forms of mental illness best helped with a combination of both. We're also discovering that the aging process can be slowed—if not reversed—with exercise and diet; speech impediments can be overcome; posture can be improved; and dyslexia can be corrected. David Myers sums it up in his textbook *Psychology*: "Our genes influence the experiences that shape us." The issue then becomes (again Myers) "not nature versus nurture, but nature *via* nurture."

No one can clarify with certainty exactly what part of our behavior is genetically based or environmentally learned. What we do know is that either way, behavior that is repeated time and time again, no matter what the cause, can be, or can appear to be, ingrained—so deeply imbedded in our being that it appears to become one with us physically. I have a friend who, when she was seventeen years old, was told that she needed glasses for reading. She had always needed glasses to see distance. She donned the reading glasses and each year found that she needed a stronger prescription. About six years later, another doctor said she had been misdiagnosed and that she did not need reading glasses at all. She told him that she couldn't read a word without them. He said, "Give it a week and you'll see fine." She did, and she could. The reason, as my opthalmologist, Dr. Barry Chaiken, explained, is that a young person who is hypermetropic, that is, far-sighted, should not be given reading glasses unless there is a medical reason to do so. Because in my friend's case there was none, the glasses had become an unwarranted crutch. Her own eyes stopped "exercising" and therefore weakened, the same way our muscles do when we remain in bed for too long. Once the "crutches" were taken away, her eyes went back "to work." It is amazing how easily the body adapts and how quickly the adaptation begins to feel "natural." This is why after years of slouching, good posture will not feel natural. Neither will walking with long strides if you've always shuffled, expressing yourself with your hands if they've always hung at your sides, leaving unclenched a heretofore intransigently clenched jaw, meeting someone's eyes if you are innately shy, or enunciating clearly if you have always slurred your words. Besides, what good is "natural" if it doesn't look good? From my vantage point, it isn't a matter of whether or not something feels natural, but whether you look better or are more effective doing it. In other words, whether what feels natural works for or against you.

One of my clients walks with a shuffle. His sons do the same. While it is possible, although highly unlikely, that their walking style stems from an inherited structural defect, it is more probable that their shuffling derives from familial mimicry. Children find their identity by copying those in authority. I remember watching my nephew, when he was a few years old, striving to emulate his father in walk and mannerisms. What effort went into this thirty-two-inch-tall child trying to stretch his legs in order to keep up with his six-foot-three dad. Should my client and his sons attempt to change their walk? My client, a writer, probably may not want or even need to. His sons, however, may feel differently. As shufflers are not generally perceived to be "go-getters," if his sons choose professions that require an appearance of gregariousness—sales, politics, marketing—they would do well to adopt a more energized gait. Will it feel natural? Not for a helluva long time. Depending on how much they work at it, though, it will certainly feel more natural—maybe even totally natural.

Much of the behavior we see in those around us appears to be so ingrained that it's hard to tell which came first, the personality or the behavior. We certainly cannot imagine the behavior disappearing without the person going through an entire personality transformation. Examples: People whose grimacing facial movements make them appear as if everything in life is difficult and painful; those who hold their head in such a way that they always appear to be looking down from their lofty perch at the rest of us; those who come across uptight and aloof because they keep their arms wrapped around their body as if they are protecting themselves from the world. Are these mannerisms manifestations of some "genetic" personality, or are they developed—"learned"—as defense mechanisms in response to events that took place outside the person's control? More to the point, does it make a difference? The answer is: Not really, because whether the behavior is genetically based or environmentally learned, whether we like it or not, our behavior is our behavior, and we are solely responsible for it. Remember Aleah of the last chapter. No matter what was rendered unto her, only she would be able to make the change. As the joke goes: "How many psychiatrists does it take to change a light bulb?" "One. But only as long as the light bulb really wants to change."

Age is not an impediment to change. Until recently speech therapists believed that past the age of twelve, accents could not be eradicated. They now find that if there's the will, an accent—or speech impediment—can be made to disappear at any age. One particular client, Howard, proved that. Talented but considered "back room" because of a lisp, Howard was never asked to be a part of his company's major client presentations. However, when his boss needed emergency surgery, Howard was the only one around who could step in. I had four days, as his boss succinctly put it, to "whip him into shape." What transpired left all of us—except Howard—speechless. Aware that not only would the client's eyes be on him, but that it would probably be his one and only chance to impress the head of the firm, Howard, intent on making an outstanding impression, spent the next four days rehearsing and working on his lisp—using the speech exercise found in chapter 7. The presentation that emerged was lisp free and captivating. Although his speech didn't feel natural, it sounded right on the tape recorder and, more than that, it sounded right to everyone else.

Whether our behavior, like Aleah's, alienates, or like Howard's, holds us back, for any of us even to want to change, our present circumstances must cause us some degree of discomfort. As Howard would testify, change can be exacting and tedious. Look at what athletes and dancers must do to develop. It makes no difference whether or not they are "naturals," possess a modicum to reasonable amounts of talent, or are only in the arena because of their parents' own unfulfilled dreams of glory. To attain professional levels of expertise, all dancers and athletes know that they must accept a nonstop physical, emotional, and mental reshaping by teachers, coaches, and the like, with the tacit understanding that demand equals potential. That is, the more demanded of you, the more promise you possess. Mollycoddling is viewed as an insult; professional criticism—sometimes constant and overbearing—is never taken as ridicule, but for what it is: I know how good you can be. Work harder (damn it!) so that you can be it!

Natural is as natural does. The more often you do it, the more natural it becomes. I was fascinated recently by a television interview of Andre Agassi, the tennis player. Talk about genetic-based versus learned behavior! His father—I am biting my tongue not to describe him in a judgmental way—put a paddle in his infant child's hand so that Andre would hit at the objects hanging over his crib. The paddle stayed with Andre as he grew into a toddler. He was told to swing at anything he wished. By the time he was four, Andre was on a tennis court hitting balls. As Agassi put it, he can't remember a time when tennis wasn't a part of his life. If he had not been born with some innate athletic ability, could he have ended up a basket case, having been forced against his "nature" to satisfy the father's own desires? Absolutely. What we do not know is if he would have been as excellent a player if he had been allowed to start at a more reasonable age—like seven or ten. He did say that he had to go through a very difficult time (at the age of eighteen) to find out why he was on a tennis court. When he decided it was for himself and the joy he got from playing, he could return to the game and win.

Hard as it is to acquire new skills, it is far more difficult to unlearn bad habits. I compare it to the difference between drawing a strong line on a clean piece of paper or on a paper that has been drawn on before. On a new one, the task is easy. One swift pass, and voilà! A clean solid line. On the used sheet, it first takes lots of erasing and then drawing the line over again and again until a strong impression is made. Howard erased his old speech and continued to work hard, so that his new enunciation now feels almost "natural." On that first day, though, he had no idea how far he could go. Neither, for that matter, did I. Nor do I with anyone who walks in my door. How can I? There are so many factors involved. Mental capacities differ, chemical makeups vary, genetic factors can produce more diversity than even a computer can compute, and then there are all those environmental influences that reshape and re-form each of the other elements.

I know an artist who rates other artists by assessing their competence (from zero talent to genius level) in different areas: the *fist,* which means technical ability, the soul, intellect, and inventiveness. By rating artists from one to ten in each category, he makes his evaluations. It never occurs to him to say that an artist is brilliant, good, mediocre, or poor. He says that one artist has a powerful fist but lacks an equally strong emotional content; another, a strong intellect and heart but a mediocre fist, and so on. He gives Picasso a ten in inventiveness and fist, an eight in intellect, and a two in heart. He feels Braque is somewhat less inventive, not as technically facile, but a lot stronger in heart and intellect. Rembrandt and Goya get his ten across the board.

I ask clients to evaluate their own presentation skills and abilities the same way, only on a scale of one to six—I omit seven through ten to leave room for improvement. You can do the same right now. At the end of the chapter is a list of the skills you will need to be an effective presenter. The **S** stands for small presentations of about one to eight people; the **L**, for nine or more. However, you may find an audience of any size filled with peers more difficult to handle than an audience filled with clients or upper management, or vice versa. Therefore, feel free to change the **S/L** to reflect situations that are more relevant to the way you react. You could replace the **S** with a **C** for client(s) and the **L** with a **P** for peers; or the **S** with an **F** for friends and the **L** with an **S** for strangers. If you're not certain how to rate yourself in some of the categories, leave the answer blank and come back to it later. I would suggest that you use a pencil so that you will have the flexibility to change your mind. Don't worry! There's no way your chart will be loaded with ones or even twos. It's impossible. If you can walk, talk, and think, you already have some ability to communicate. Besides, facility alone has never assured a strong performance.

Remember: Skills Can Be Developed into Talent; Talent Not Developed Disintegrates.

In my experience there are two kinds of students: those who rely on facility rather than sweat and those who sweat to become facile. It is the latter group whose talents bloom. None of us burst from the womb able to speak with a mellifluous voice, enunciate clearly, and make dramatic use of our eyes and facial expressions, not to mention being able to control any or all other portions of our bodies. We acquired whatever skills we do have, and we can always acquire more. This is why even a "natural" such as Laurence Olivier studied acting, Picasso studied painting, Stravinsky studied music, Martha Graham studied dance, and obviously Andre Agassi studied tennis.

"SPEAK UP!" PRESENTATION SKILLS LIST

Rate yourself 1–6 on each skill. (6 is the highest.)
S = presentations of 1–8 people; L = 9 or more.
Feel free to change S/L to reflect presentations to
friends vs. strangers or peers vs. upper management.

PART I: PRESENTATION OF SELF

1. Presence

S	L	
___	___	Energize self.
___	___	Control energy.
___	___	Appear confident.
___	___	Listen attentively.
___	___	Appear to listen attentively.
___	___	"Infect" audience.
___	___	Present cohesive appearance.

2. Eye Contact

Ability to:

S	L	
___	___	Read audience one person at a time.
___	___	Move in seemingly random pattern.
___	___	Move from one person to another at end of a word, phrase, or sentence.
___	___	Move off a mesmerizing face.

3. Expression

Ability to:

S	L	
___	___	Be facially mobile.
___	___	Stay facially expressive.
___	___	Expressions correspond to ideas.
___	___	Expressions emphasize emotions.

S	L	
___	___	Smile with eyes.
___	___	Smile with mouth.

4. Posture

Ability to:

___	___	Maintain a comfortable, erect stance.
___	___	Expanded rib cage.
___	___	Relaxed arms.
___	___	Stretched spinal column.

___	___	Maintain a comfortable, erect, seated position.
___	___	Expanded rib cage.
___	___	Active arms.
___	___	Stretched spinal column.
___	___	Toes directly ahead.

5. Gestures

Ability to:

___	___	Control fingers, hands, and arms to accent ideas.
___	___	Keep hands open, unclasped, away from crotch, out of pockets, in front of body.
___	___	Keep arms uncrossed.
___	___	Keep elbows away from body.

6. Body Movements

Ability to:

___	___	Control body movements.
___	___	Walk and stop at will.
___	___	Avoid disconcerting mannerisms, i.e., twitching, rocking, weaving, scratching.

7. Voice & Diction

Ability to:

___	___	Speak without breathiness, stridency, nasality, throatiness, or hoarseness.

	S	L	
	___	___	Speak with appropriate volume.
	___	___	Speak with wide range of tonality.
	___	___	Modulate pacing.
	___	___	Speak with clear, precise, unforced enunciation.
	___	___	Pause for effect.
	___	___	Control breathing.

8. Rehearsals

Ability to: ___   ___   Rehearse without becoming stale.

PART II : PRESENTATION OF IDEAS

Ability to:	___	___	Articulate thoughts in a clear and concise manner.
	___	___	Construct a talk with a beginning, middle, and an end.
	___	___	Meet needs of audience.
	___	___	Change course midstream (think on your feet).
	___	___	Keep audience involved.
	___	___	Speak extemporaneously.
	___	___	Write for speaking.

PART III: PRESENTATION OF MATERIALS

Ability to:	___	___	Construct visually arresting materials that enhance ideas.
	___	___	Write succinct, **active** bullets for visuals.
	___	___	Use visual aids with ease.

LAST BUT NOT LEAST

Ability to: ___   ___   **ENJOY YOURSELF** as you present!

Chapter 3

Misconception: "Everyone's looking at me."

I often ask clients what all entrances have in common. I explain that an entrance can be anything from standing up in place to speak, to walking to the head of a conference table to present, to getting up to take the podium, to entering a room in which you do not know a soul, to entering one in which you do. The answers always go something like: "It's the moment people first notice you." "It's your audience's first impression of you." "It's a way to get attention." And the ever-present: "Everyone is looking at you." What fascinates me about these responses is that none takes into consideration the action of the person making the entrance. The answers refer only to the behavior of the supposed audience, even though not all the situations I describe entail an audience. That room in which we may not know a soul could just as easily be a cocktail party or professional gathering as an auditorium in which we're to be the designated speaker. To attract attention in such a room, nowadays, we'd probably have to be nude, this year's celebrity, or Elvis Presley incarnate. More to my point, even if we were the speaker, most audiences would barely give us more than a perfunctory glance until we opened our mouth to speak—and sometimes not even then. Audiences need time to reorient themselves; to leave the conversation with the person seated next to them; to stop thinking of what they must do when the session ends; to put out of mind the phone calls they must make or the problems at home. No. The answers I would wish to hear about what all entrances have, or should have, in common are: 1) They all involve movement, that is, you move from here to there; and 2) they involve a destination, the entrant's destination—your destination if you are the one making an entrance.

While I may rarely get the answers I'm looking for, the answers I do get certainly describe how many people feel when they are asked to get up to speak or when they are put in a situation in which they believe they have become the center of attention. It's how everyone of us can feel when we worry about what others think of us. It is not simply that we experience an overwhelming sensation that all eyes are on us, but we become convinced that behind each pair of eyes sits a judge assessing, scrutinizing, and evaluating our every move.

I am not saying that there aren't those people who delight in scrutinizing others, but whether or not they exist is not the issue. The issue is what you are doing when you enter a room, or give a presentation, or simply try to communicate with others. If you are not looking to see where you are going, if you are not concentrated on your audience or on others around you, if you are not focused outside yourself, then you must be focused on yourself. Just as we cannot bat and pitch simultaneously, none of us can focus outside and in at the same time, which means that if you are concentrated on yourself, then those eyes you feel on you must be yours and yours alone. Your eyes are making that assessment. Your eyes are judging your performance. We could call this an out-of-body experience: We leave our bodies where they are and mentally stand outside to see how we're doing. We accomplish this feat, this act of being in two places at once, by inadvertently turning our audience into mirrors; we see them not as who they are, but as reflections of our own thoughts and feelings about how we view ourselves.

Much the same way that the last two chapters overlapped, so do this and the following one. These also build on what was previously discussed: our sense of self. However, this chapter centers on how a faulty sense of self can inhibit our ability to view people, situations, and our self objectively, and it explains what we can do to overcome the problem so that we can learn to "read" audiences with an objective eye. The next chapter explains how an absence of self can form a "grandiose personality" and how insecurity in general can provoke, even in nongrandiose personalities, some rather grandiose behavior that can be extremely self-defeating, such as the person who behaves in a grandiose manner ends up refusing to take those very actions that would allow him or her to become more secure.

When we worry about what others think of us, we are unable to assess their behavior or decide how we feel about them.

Mary Ann. Imagine being in a situation in which another person displays behavior that, to put it mildly, is slightly bizarre, and instead of viewing the behavior as odd, you not only accept it as "normal" but allow it to intimidate you. This happened to four individuals (two men, two women) who attended a workshop I gave a few years ago. The intimidator was the fifth participant who, ostensibly, had decided to attend the workshop in order to "check it out" for other people in her company. We'll call her Mary Ann. When I first met Mary Ann in her office, I remember thinking that she reminded me of a porcelain doll, although she did not exhibit any of the strange behavior to which we were later exposed. Then, on the day of the workshop, whereas the others arrived on time, Mary Ann came late. The others, per my request, dressed casually to facilitate an open, relaxed environment; Mary Ann dressed up. Her clothes—closer to evening than to business attire—fit as if they had been made on her. Her makeup was exactingly applied. Her hair, meticulously knotted, had not a hair out of place. To add to the picture, she was stunning. At the time of the workshop she grossed in the six figures; however, the other participants were no slouches, either. They were: a lawyer, an advertising account executive, a public relations writer, and a financial advisor—all highly successful individuals. Throughout the day Mary Ann's demeanor remained aloof, and her behavior grew increasingly odd—perhaps because she was no longer in control or in an environment that she could control, as she had been in her own office. She made constant trips to the bathroom, emerging each time with her hair in a radically different style: loose, knotted, braided, pushed to one side, then to the other. Complaining of chapped lips, she continually pulled out a mirror and reapplied her lipstick as if Chap Stick had never been invented. Her speech, already studied, became more so—her obvious need for perfection so all-consuming that she appeared to craft each sentence as if one mistake would cause her to dissolve into nothingness. As amazed by her behavior as I was, I was more surprised by that of the others, none of whom appeared to find hers out of the ordinary. In fact, they treated her quite deferentially. When I spoke later with the four separately, they all said that they had noticed the hair and the lipstick but had not "thought about it." They also said that they had accepted her remoteness as a perfectly logical reaction to their own "obvious inadequacies," or as a result of "her professionalism and our lack of it" or "reasonable under the circumstances." These were extraordinary responses from such a seasoned group.

Mary Ann's own story was one of survival. She came from a highly demanding father who strove for perfection in himself and in Mary Ann—an ideal that he must have decided he couldn't attain, as he committed suicide when she was six. After his death, her mother, disliking the caretaker role, reinforced his perfectionism by reiterating that Mary Ann was her "wonderfully perfect baby who *thankfully* never cried," thus insuring that Mary Ann never would. Unable to confront a ghost who had deserted her and living with a nonnurturing, nonprotective mother, Mary Ann maintained the memory of the "good" father by attempting to live up to his fantasy. While this may not excuse Mary Ann's behavior, it certainly explains it, but what about the group's responses? Why were they not able to recognize her preening as a symptom of a disturbed personality? And why did they focus on her aloofness and, to a person, accept her aloofness as "reasonable under the circumstances"?

First, their defenses were down. Each of the four had come to the workshop intending to improve upon his or her own presentation style, which meant that they all believed there was something that needed improving. Second, there was the issue of dress. Although where clothes are concerned the majority usually rules, in this instance, because the group was already feeling a bit insecure, Mary Ann's walking in suited to the nines exacerbated those feelings. Third, there was the strangeness of Mary Ann's behavior. We can all experience feelings of discomfort when someone exhibits strange behavior. The problem here was that the members of this group allowed that discomfort to get entangled with their own sense of self, and none of them felt secure enough to take her- or himself out of the situation and look at Mary Ann objectively. Instead, they saw themselves through what they assumed were her eyes, even though she wasn't even aware they were there. In other words, they used Mary Ann as a mirror in which to see themselves just as she used a real mirror to reassure herself that she was intact.

Mirrors

Basically, there are three types of mirrors: 1) glass/metal and the like; 2) people; and 3) the imagined variety. *Glass mirrors,* generally, are made of plate glass coated with a reflective surface. Where the glass and the reflector meet is called the mirror line. When the materials are of a high enough quality so that all distortion is eliminated, if our vision is not clouded (either literally or figuratively), like it or not, what we see is what is there. *People mirrors* are just that: people—people who, in our early childhood, give us our identity; and people in whom we, as adults, recognize aspects of our own personality. *Imagined mirrors* are the mirrors we create when we project onto either the glass or adult people-mirrors what we feel about ourselves. In other words, we judge ourselves based on what we presume others think of us—presumptions that usually form through our interactions with our early childhood people mirrors. Like the glass mirror, imagined mirrors also have a mirror line; however, here it is the wall we erect when we no longer can see our audience because we are too busy looking at ourselves.

People Mirrors: The Early Childhood Variety

The psychologist D. W. Winnicott suggests that "the precursor of the mirror is the mother's face." Although Winnicott makes it clear that he is referring to sighted children only (and that the voice and handling make up for the face in nonsighted children), he is saying that whether the person is our mother or another, whatever we perceive to be our primary caretaker's reaction to us will profoundly effect how we feel about ourselves and how, as we grow, we will present our self—be it to a mirror or to another person. In *The Interpersonal World of the Infant,* Daniel Stern explains how this parental "mirroring" is enacted through the parent's facial expressions, physical interactions, and vocal insinuations—what Stern terms "attunement"— the "tool" through which the parent or caretaker lets the child know that the parent understands and either approves or disapproves of what the infant feels. For instance, the child giggles, the parent giggles; the child gets happier, the parent gets happier; the child coos, the parent "gitchigitchigoo"s. In this interaction the parent lets the child know that the parent understands that the child feels happy and that the child's happiness makes the parent happy. If, however, the child giggles and the parent looks disapprovingly or doesn't react at all, the child learns that what the child expresses is bad. Although Stern uses a number of case studies to explain how we are all programmed by our parent's "desires, fears, prohibitions and fantasies," the example that fascinated me the most was that of Sam and his mother, related here in a much condensed version. According to Stern, the mother was observed always just to undermatch the intensity of her son Sam's play. For instance, when he giggled and excitedly flapped his arms, she pleasantly smiled and rather stolidly said, "Yes, honey," a response that did not fit her normal highly animated style of behavior. After much probing from Stern, the mother admitted that she purposely undermatched her son's intensity; she did so because she didn't wish him to turn out like his father, a rather passive man. In other words, she was "programming" her child. However, if this programming had continued, it would have had the opposite effect than the one the mother wanted, because the mother had mistakenly assumed that if she underplayed her own personality, Sam's would be forced to blossom. In Stern's words, "one of the fascinating paradoxes is that . . . it would do exactly the opposite of what she intended. Her underattunements would tend to create a lower-keyed child . . . more like the father."

We now know that some of our basic neural pathways, that is, our synapses, are being laid down during the first twelve months of life and that touching, caressing, rocking, smiling, cooing, and adoring eyes not only will influence the brain's wiring, but also will promote the emotional, mental, and physical growth of the child. Of course, anything can go wrong during this period. The mother or primary caretaker may be misguided, as in Sam's case. The mother may be called away to nurse a parent or another child in a hospital. The child may develop an illness that interferes with this interplay. In the most extreme cases, the child may receive no parenting of any kind, as in the case of children of drug addicts, or what has recently happened to the children left to rot in Romanian orphanages. We just need to look at pictures of these orphanage children to understand what effects neglect or an inappropriate or complete lack of attunement can have on a child. Ten-year-old children who are no bigger than three-year-olds, children who cannot smile, children who rock themselves incessantly—these children seem to confirm an old story told about a ruler of Sicily who, in order to test his pet theory regarding a common birth language, took newborn infants away from their natural mothers, giving them to foster ones. The latter were ordered only to tend to the babies' physical needs, but not to speak to or smile at or "love" them. According to the legend, Frederick never got to check out his theory on language, as all one hundred children died from emotional neglect long before they could speak.

While we may not have experienced anything this extreme, few if any of us come from perfect environments. Life usually interferes even when parents have the best of intentions. Because children assume that they are the center of the universe and that all a parent feels must relate to them, children base their own feelings of self-worth on what they believe their parents' feelings toward them to be. For instance, small children who, simply by their presence, can light up a parent's face will approach a mirror with glee. "That's me!" they will say as they point and giggle away at their image reflected, "Me!" On the other hand, children of nonsmiling or disapproving caregivers tend to assume that they are a huge disappointment even when this may not be the case. If a parent is sad, the child will assume (albeit on a sensory, not a cognitive level) that he or she is the root cause of the parent's sadness. If the sadness persists (perhaps the parent suffers from chronic depression), the toddler will incorporate that sadness into his or her own feelings of self-worth. Children of these parents receive a double whammy. Physically they do not smile because they are not smiled at, and emotionally they cannot smile because they have incorporated what they perceive to be their parents' attitudes toward them into their own attitude about themselves. For many of these children looking into a mirror is agonizing, because what they see reflected back is quite literally a noninviting personality, a sad sack.

While grandparents, siblings, teachers, nannies, and the like—our other childhood mirrors—may modify parental reactions, more often they end up substantiating them. The reason for this is that a happy child does make others smile, which reinforces the child's positive feelings, whereas the unhappy child is most often approached with pity—if, that is, he or she is approached at all—confirming what the child already believes to be the case: that he or she certainly is not loveable or possibly not even worthwhile. All this is by way of explaining that cohesive, confident selves do not come easily. Because of this, many people find themselves projecting onto adult people mirrors and glass mirrors images that may not be accurate at all.

Glass Mirrors

One would assume that if two people stood in front of the same mirror, they would both see the same thing. They don't. They both project onto the image in front of them their individual attitudes, preconceived ideas, and mood—the same components that color every piece of information we take in. This explains why an anorectic sees her (or in some cases, his) reflection as that of someone exceedingly overweight, while we view the anorectic as a skeletal figure. It explains why, on a particular day when we may not feel too secure, a pimple or blemish can appear to take over our entire face, or our hairline seems to be receding in inches rather than millimeters. It also explains how someone who, by society's standards, may not be attractive, can see reflected an attractive individual (a product of early positive reinforcement), whereas someone like Mary Ann, whose looks are astounding, can see only imperfection. Mary Ann's story reminds me of another client who credits glass mirrors with helping her manage to struggle through a childhood filled with parental neglect. It seems that as a young girl she stared into every mirror she passed in order assure herself that she existed. She would smile into each mirror, desperate for the image that stared back to be a beautiful maiden whose looks could melt the world, or, more accurately, her parents' eyes. It took years, in addition to lots of professional help, for her to leave these mirrors and engage other people, seeing them for what they are rather than what she needed them to be, a validation of her own existence.

Imagined Mirrors

Again, imagined mirrors are those onto which we project what we think others think of us, based on how we see ourselves, which most likely is based on how we believe our parents saw (or didn't see) us. "Ted," the character played by Ted Knight on *The Mary Tyler Moore Show,* is a perfect example of an imagined mirror watcher. When he looked into another character's face, we knew his foremost concern was how he, Ted Baxter, was being seen. When he looked directly into the camera, it was his own reflection he sought; the audience, his audience—Mary, Lou, Murray, the camera—existed for the sole purpose of giving Ted approval (the approval he must never have gotten in early childhood). Ted turned everyone and everything into a mirror. His behavior would be described by psychologists as narcissistic. *Narcissism* derives from the Greek myth about a beautiful young man who is totally indifferent to others. When he refuses all offers of love, including that of Echo, a mountain nymph, he is made to fall in love with his own image reflected in a mountain pool. Unable to possess the image, he eventually wastes away from unrequited desire and is transformed into the flower narcissus—a showy flower at the end of a lone stalk.

Now here's where things get a bit complicated. There is good and bad narcissism, as Kohut, the father of Self Psychology would characterize it, healthy and pathological narcissism, as well as all that goes between. Obviously, Ted Baxter's narcissism would not be considered healthy. His fits the description of narcissistic personalities, as described in Jerome Levin's interpretation of Otto Kernberg's theories, as people who "typically relate to others not as separate people, but as an extension of themselves." On the other hand, healthy narcissism is described as a reasonable appreciation of oneself—when we know our self-worth, when we value who we are, and when we do not exaggerate our sense of self. A person who possesses a sufficient dose of healthy narcissism does not need to put others down in order to feel better; does not need constant affirmation of his or her worth; may very well enjoy taking center stage, but is not driven by a desire or craving to be the center of attention. Of course there's more to it, but without going into an entire psychological treatise, this description, albeit short, should suffice for our purposes. What we need to remember is that even the healthiest among us can behave in a narcissistic manner at one time or another. It is certainly how all of us behave when we turn our audience into extensions of ourselves, in other words, when we stand in front of any audience (whether that audience is comprised of one or one thousand) and worry about ourselves, thereby causing us to behave in a highly self-conscious manner.

Self-Conscious vs. Shy Behavior

Interestingly, the narcissist and the shy person are really flip sides of the same coin, as both, in their own ways, erect walls that prevent them from fully interacting with other people. Shyness has been defined as self-consciousness, timidity, bashfulness, and diffidence. People who suffer from it—and it is a condition to suffer from—have been labeled mousey to aloof. Current research shows that some forms of shyness can be inherited, but for the most part, it is often introduced or reinforced culturally and societally. Whether it is experienced as a minor encumbrance or a highly debilitating condition, shyness may be treated behav-

iorally, psychologically or a combination of both—
depending on the particular root cause. Yet, although
the adjectives *self-conscious* and *shy* are often used inter-
changeably, we tend to have a kindlier response to
someone whom we consider shy than to someone we
think of as being self-conscious. While the psychotherapist would say that there are taints of narcissism in both shy and self-conscious people, those
who are painfully shy really do not wish to call
attention to themselves and do so unwittingly,
whereas those who behave in a self-conscious manner
appear to be screaming for recognition. There exists
one other important difference between the two.
While the narcissist may fly into a rage or sink into a
depression at the thought that he or she is not the only
person to feel a certain way—that he or she is not
"special"—shy people find relief at discovering that
they are not alone in their shyness.

Lisa/Jim. I first met Lisa at a luncheon where I was
the guest speaker. What I noticed, before and during
my talk, was the look of trepidation that never left her
eyes. When I could engage her, it took but seconds
before her eyes darted away. Later when she called to
sign up for a workshop, I was both impressed by her
willingness to confront the problem and pleased to be
given the chance to help. Attending the same workshop
was Jim, a perceptive, bright, and extremely attractive
young man whose lack of facial expression I found
most disconcerting. When he was silent he appeared
vacuous; when he spoke, although his words demon-
strated his involvement, his bland expression belied it.
Each workshop participant is normally given specific
tasks to work on throughout the day that relate specif-

ically to the individual participant's needs. In this workshop I asked Lisa to make persistent eye contact with the other attendees, and I asked Jim to move his facial muscles even if the movements held no particular meaning.

I expected Lisa to have trouble, as eye contact can be both psychologically and physically painful for the extremely shy person—physically, because her eye muscles, which had been in the habit of darting, would now have to be retrained to hold her eyes in place; psychologically, because engaging another human being went against her grain. However, as she was obviously trying, I allowed her much leeway. On the other hand, I had no doubt that Jim could do much more and was curious as to what was holding him back. Throwing caution to the wind, I asked if he was aware of how attractive he was. Red-faced, he managed a slight affirmative nod. I inquired if his good looks embarrassed him, and did he think that by remaining expressionless he could play them down? For the first time that day, Lisa actually looked at someone with no awareness of herself. Her jaw fell open as Jim managed a soft "yes." Later she confided that although she had been told that attractive, intelligent people, who seemed to have it all, could feel self-conscious, until that moment, she hadn't believed it. With the ice broken, the other participants admitted that when Jim kept his face in repose, he came across as conceited, and that once he allowed himself to be physically expressive, they all felt more comfortable with him.

Regrettably, revelations, no matter how enlightening, rarely produce immediate physical changes. It takes time to undo what has become habit. However, from that point on, both Jim and Lisa were able to practice unencumbered. Jim worked hard to be animated. In the beginning, he said it felt, and, in truth, even looked, forced; however, eventually he was able to internalize the movements until they became natural to him. Lisa continued working on her eye contact, spending an allotted amount of time each day practicing the eye exercises shown on the next page. Both realized that their eyes had been trained on themselves. As another client, who also suffered from a similar syndrome, put it, "I had no idea that in trying to protect myself, I was, in actuality, acting rude to everyone else."

It is rude to turn other people into mirrors. It also deprives you of the ability to see who they really are—not who you imagine them to be. Now there is, as we shall see in the chapter on rehearsing, a time and place for mirrors—the glass kind—but it is not when you are in front of an audience. In front of an audience all mirrors must be put away so that you can see with a clear eye. As with all the skills presented in this book, you need to tackle this one both physically and psychologically in order to master them.

The Physical Aspects of Good Eye Contact

Most people have no idea whether or not their eye contact is poor, fair, good, or excellent. Many assume that as long as they make some contact with another person's eyes, no matter how fleeting, eye contact has been achieved. While that might be true in the literal sense, it has nothing to do with what I consider to be true eye contact. You need not only to meet the eyes of your audience, you must see your audience. To do this you must first train your eyes to work in perfect synchronization with your words.

EXERCISE:

1) Get a box of solid white notebook paper reinforcements and stick them around the room to represent the eyes in an audience. For instance, put two on a lamp, two more on the wall, two more on books in the book shelf and so on.

2) Using the sentence, "Good morning! My name is _____ and yours is . . . ?", begin saying the first syllable to the first set of "eyes," skip over to the other side of the room for the second syllable, then to another set of eyes for the third syllable. Keep going until the sentence is finished. Obviously, you can make up sentences of your own. Stay with one syllable at a time until you have this aspect of the exercise under your control. Move slowly enough so that each sound of the syllable is pronounced.

Important: Do not leave a pair of eyes before the last sound of the syllable has been fully made. Practice taking a beat before you leave to go on to the next pair of eyes. You might want to ask someone to watch you as you perform the exercise to make certain that you do not inadvertently leave a pair of eyes before you have finished the last sound of the syllable.

3) As you progress, practice with two syllables, then three, then four.
4) Once you've mastered the above, practice alternating between words and phrases.

Keep in mind that passing your eyes over an audience or moving in the midst of a word or thought is like passing a tray of food around a cocktail party and not letting anyone get a morsel. The idea here is to watch your audience "swallow" your words.

Be certain that you don't move in consecutive order around the room. This practice of moving in a pattern becomes predictable, and your audience knows when to expect you to land on them, which inadvertently allows them mentally to wander off. It is best to reach out to the person farthest from you first, then to the person nearest you second, then back again to the far side, then to the near side working your way through the middle (see diagram).

The audience

	5	20	1	21	3	
	14	10			19	7
		8		17		13
	22		16		9	15
		13		12		23
8			14		6	
		2	11		18	4

The speaker

Obviously, the more you practice the skill in your everyday life, the easier it will be to carry out in front of an audience. Remember, there's no magic wand like the one Gerald, a lawyer in his fifties, expected. He came to me because, as he described it, he was suddenly battling heightened anxieties whenever he was faced with the prospect of having to speak to audiences of any size. I suggested he attend a workshop. What quickly became apparent was that his eye contact was so bad that he had to feel extraordinarily disassociated from his audience. He certainly managed to absent himself from the workshop. He looked out windows, up at the ceiling, down at the floor—anywhere he could mentally remove himself. Clearly he had long ago decided that if something made him uncomfortable, he would leave—one way or another. By the middle of the day, I had dubbed him "the helium balloon." My sense that his behavior was longstanding and not a recent occurrence was substantiated when he mentioned, as if he were proud of the fact, that his kindergarten teachers had labeled him peripatetic. He also informed us that any kind of confrontation unnerved him and always had. Needless to say, it was amazing that he had survived in his profession for this long. I tried all day to get him to practice looking at others, but he quickly let me know that he had come for and had expected that I would give him some incantation that could reach deep into his psyche and turn his world around. He didn't want to accept that while I couldn't repair his internal damage, he could have developed a skill that would have lessened his anxiety.

Allan was a different story. He, too, had eyes that drifted off, but he wanted to change and understood the physical and mental work required to do so. Like Lisa, he forced his eyes to "attach" to his audience and forced himself to push through the mirror line he had erected over the years. What he found, as many people do, was that this attachment grounded him and helped eradicate whatever anxieties existed. Without that attachment he had felt detached, weightless, alone—a condition that exacerbated the discomfort he was already experiencing.

Again, to read an audience you must keep a constant eye on each member of the audience. You may not scan! Your eyes must penetrate your listeners' eyes without making them uncomfortable. Your eyes must constantly move from person to person (never in consecutive order) and should remain on each person for a full word, phrase, or sentence.

The Psychological Aspects of Good Eye Contact

Good eye contact begins with your intent. If your intent is to get the audience to focus on you, your eye contact will be narcissistic and off-putting. If however, your intent is to watch your audience in order to determine how it is taking in the information you are presenting, if your intent is to see whether or not your audience understands what is being said, if your intent is to see if your audience needs to hear a fuller explanation, if your intent is to see if it, as a whole or individually, appears to disagree or agree with what you are saying—then your eye contact will be right on the mark. It is your job to ascertain if and how your listeners listen and to do so as you speak. Some listeners take in everything while appearing not to; others' thoughts are elsewhere, yet they are able to fake concentration. Your job is to discover which is which, to watch to see if your listeners are taking issue with what you are saying. If you do not address concerns immediately, your audiences' ability to take in any additional information will be blocked as they silently wrestle with what you have said. Audiences can also have short attention spans. You may have to change the way you deliver your message to meet your audience's listening capabilities. Of course, to do any of this you must remain flexible, which means you must know your material, pay close attention, and remain *objective* by depersonalizing the situation. A slight digression:

Objectivity: To show clients how to approach a situation of any kind with objectivity, I use a visualization exercise that employs the simplest tool: a legal pad. Here are two examples that, while not about making presentations, show how the exercise works.

Example 1: Bruce came to me because whenever his boss entered his office he found himself freezing in terror. His boss could fly into unexpected rages. Bruce found himself taking these rages personally even though he knew that everyone, including himself, believed them to be his boss's way of keeping his own creative juices flowing. I showed Bruce a legal pad and told him to imagine that it was his boss's fury. Then I shoved it at him, yelling at him while I did. He quickly grabbed the pad and pulled it toward himself. I took it back and told him that this time, after I flung it at him, to get rid of it. This time he flung it back at me. I explained that both times he had personalized the anger, first by holding on to the pad, and the second time by turning it into a pawn to be passed back and forth between us. I asked that the next time I yelled and shoved the pad toward him he take it and place it on a table in front of both of us. It took a number of tries, but eventually Bruce was able to distance himself from the representation of his boss's rage. Obviously the trick was to translate the experience to real life. It took a bit of practice, but eventually it worked. Bruce began to be able to judge whether his boss's rage was simply one of his "fixes" or if it was a problem that both he and his boss needed to solve.

Keep in mind that to be objective does not mean to disavow responsibility. A sad child is not attractive. Jim did come across as "just another pretty face." And, Lisa's behavior was "mousey." In other words, if Bruce were justifiably the cause of his boss's anger, then he would have to acknowledge the problem and deal with it. Even so, he would have to remind himself that his boss's anger was at something Bruce had done, rather than at Bruce himself.

Example 2: An assistant to the head of a small company, Dot called me in a highly agitated state. A fellow employee had informed her that Dot's boss had given him a raise, saying that although it was modest, the employee should be grateful, as Dot hadn't had one in years. Dot felt betrayed. She saw this as a breach of confidentiality and a personal assault on her integrity. Feeling too wounded to confront her boss, she allowed her hurt to fester. Not wanting to quit a job she needed and loved, wisely she sought help.

At our first meeting Dot interrupted my questions with a stream of "buts." "But he should have known better." "But I've been so loyal! How could he have done such a thing?" And the most telling "but": "But he knows I haven't asked for a raise because times are tough."

Again, pad of paper in hand, I asked her to remove herself from the situation and look at it from a distance. She had to look at the pad not only from where she stood but from her boss's perspective as well. Slowly she began to realize that 1) her boss may have been attempting to minimize his own inability to pay and that his remark had nothing whatsoever to do with her; 2) that because she had not discussed the reason she had not asked him for a raise, he could not know that she'd been playing the martyr; 3) that she needed to separate her own raise from her reaction to his remark; and 4) that my questions hadn't implied that her boss's actions were justifiable, just that she wasn't part of his equation. Once she had disentangled herself from the issues, she was able to strategize an approach. She went to her boss and explained that although she understood he hadn't meant any harm, his discussing her salary situation with another employee had undermined her position as well as sowing seeds of distrust; if he discussed her with another employee, the other employee could logically assume he might someday be discussed as well. Her boss apologized profusely, explaining that his comments had emanated from a desire to make the raise seem larger than it was. With the air cleared, she brought up her own raise, and they agreed on a figure.

You can also use the same technique. Take a legal pad and imagine that it represents the content of your presentation. Now imagine yourself walking around a room handing out sheets of the paper to different members of the audience. If you really focus on giving the paper to the audience, you will begin to see the audience as receivers of your message, not as judge and jury of your performance. Keep in mind that a knotted brow on someone in an audience can denote confusion or a headache; a startled look, an expression of surprise or an attack of gas; a blank stare, boredom or the manner in which someone takes in information (as discussed in chapter 5: "Everyone can see what I'm feeling").

Again, if you concentrate on getting your message across, if you concern yourself with how others are receiving that message and not how they are receiving you, you will be free to inquire or respond to your audience's facial reactions, whatever they might be. Of course, if your audience appears bored, you might, just might, be boring, or your audience could be exhibiting drowsiness due to poor ventilation. Whatever the problem, by keeping an eye on your audience you are free to ask whether you've made yourself clear, whether your audience may have concerns about what you've said that need to be addressed, or simply whether you need to open a window or call for the electrician. While some people fool themselves into believing they are mesmerizing their audience, and in doing so, make fools of themselves, most of us judge ourselves much more harshly than any audience can. What my clients have discovered over and over again is, that by keeping an honest eye on an audience, they see exactly how the audience listens, and they can respond appropriately and, in turn, develop an honest rapport. It makes not only their audiences comfortable, but themselves as well.

Once again, only because this cannot be said often enough: **To be effective in all your presentations you need to concentrate on how and if others are receiving your message—not on how they are receiving you!**

CHAPTER 4

Misconception: "I just need to believe in myself and I'll develop confidence."

Over and over again the calls come in: "I'm sending you so-and-so. Need you to build up their confidence." Or "I know if I just looked more confident, I'd be more successful." And this chapter's misconception: "I just need to believe in myself and I'll develop confidence." Oh, that overused word: *confidence*. An extraordinary quality exhibited by those lucky souls who can stride into any room and look perfectly at ease with themselves and those around them. No need for them to court attention; they command it by simply being.

Confidence. We admire it. We envy it. We want it. And we often go to great lengths to camouflage its loss or lack. There is nothing wrong with doing so. Whistling a happy tune worked for Anna with her king in Siam. Bluffing can and should help us through anxiety provoking situations. Should and can . . . at least, initially. Although bluffs often offer unseen mantles of protection, they have limited life spans. It is the rare con man or woman who can sustain a bluff for any prolonged length of time. For the rest of us, one of two things occur when we "fake it." Either we attempt to camouflage our lack of skill or knowledge with an inflation of ego, swaggering more and more grandly until someone almost feels obliged to call our bluff, or the conscious or subconscious knowledge that we are bluffing insidiously gnaws away at us until our facade crumbles and we turn into mumbling ninnies. No, when a bluff's time is up, it's up, leaving the bluffer more than a little exposed.

As already stated, confidence comes from three things and three things only: 1) knowing what to do, 2) learning how to do it, and 3) doing it often enough so that you can do it with confidence. Confidence cannot and does not spring from magic wands and wishful thinking, no matter what the current school of self-esteem-building purports. You know the one. The "I say you are, therefore, you are what I say" and "Keep repeating what you wish to be often enough and you'll become" espoused by pop psychologists and too many educators who should know better. I beg to differ with them all.

Once again, we cannot be anything we want to be. We can learn a variety of skills, improve on the ones we have, be better than we are, but we cannot be anything we wish. Those who preach otherwise render enormous damage to the psyches of their flock. Peter Pan may have gotten Wendy and crew to take off with magic dust and faith, but for the rest of us stranded in reality, we can repeat "I can fly" from now until doomsday, even wildly flap our arms, and we will still fall with a splat if we're gullible enough to leap off into space.

It is not that I'm against all mantras. Repeating "I can, I can, I can" may be quite useful in overcoming the anxieties we experience as we learn a new skill or confront a new situation, but blind faith and desire alone cannot and will not achieve results. Anyone who believes otherwise is bound to be gravely disappointed. Janet certainly was.

Janet. A young sales trainee had begged her boss to let her attend a workshop. She signed up telling me how she couldn't wait. However, once she was in, she erected wall after wall to keep constructive criticism away. Obviously, each bit of criticism was received as inflicted shame. She built her first wall after I requested that she take her feet off the sofa where she had plopped cross-legged, shoes and all. The next wall went up when the group commented that sitting with one leg curled up under her was not proper business etiquette. The final, and ultimately insurmountable, wall arose when I remarked that she "needn't leave herself at home." What I meant was that when she stood to present, she didn't have to turn herself into someone or something she was not (discussed further in chapter 8). Heard correctly, this is a compliment. How Janet heard it, I'll never know. She shut down completely. She refused to return for the follow-up sessions, would not take my telephone calls or answer my letter. I asked one of her co-workers to intervene. He reported back that Janet was "furious" with me because she "had come for esteem building" and I "had spent the entire time working on her skills." I *had* worked on her skills, and by doing so I had exposed inadequacies that had brought on shame. If she had made clear to me her goals before she came, I would have told her that I could not give, or teach, self-esteem. All I could do was teach her skills, which when learned, could lead her to feel truly confident in her ability to present herself and her material effectively. Nothing more. Nothing less.

It is important that we do not confuse confidence with self-esteem. We can have a strong sense of self and not feel confident in a particular area. By the same token, we may be confident in our ability to perform a specific task or tasks and suffer from incredibly low self-esteem.

Self-esteem CANNOT be taught! Self-esteem should develop naturally in childhood. Under normal enough circumstances and with good enough parenting, we should arrive at adulthood with a reasonable amount of self-esteem in place. Once grown, we can enhance or further develop whatever self-esteem we lack; however, we can only do so provided that a reasonable amount of self-esteem already exists. Considering Janet's extreme reaction, a far more rehabilitative approach with a great deal of internal reparative work would appear to be required for her to develop the belief in herself she craves.

This said, had Janet stuck around and mastered the skills she needed, she could have gained confidence in her ability to present. This then might have led to her feeling better about herself as both her work and personal life improved. Sadly, the concept that mastery can lead to confidence that, in turn, can evolve into pride at one's accomplishments, had eluded Janet completely. It eludes all too many others as well.

George. A partner in a public relations firm, George had no problems giving presentations; it was his three partners who had problems with the way he gave them. As they described it, if George didn't get an immediate reaction from his audience—and most people on the receiving end of a new business pitch work hard at remaining visually neutral—he would ram his point in over and over and over again. Not a great way to win clients and influence the decision-making process. The partners and I decided that in order for George not to feel singled out, it would be more diplomatic if they were to suggest that they all get critiqued by a professional. When they brought it up to George, he told them they were crazy. They could get help, but he certainly didn't need any. With that he stalked out of the meeting, never to discuss the subject again.

Lewis, a marketing executive, was a sometime presenter. Sometimes he was great; sometimes not. He did, however, have an excuse for every failure: a bad mood, a client he didn't care about, a bad hair day. After a particularly disastrous presentation, he finally decided to seek help in becoming more consistent. However, he insisted on private sessions, emphatically refusing a workshop situation from which he could have reaped many more benefits. I had to terminate our sessions early on, because Lewis absolutely refused to stand and practice a presentation in front of me. He insisted that all he needed was to be given tips and he would "get it." He didn't.

Caroline. A strong employment record as well as a highly assertive presentation of self during the interviewing process had gotten Caroline hired. A formal meeting with upper management in which she had come across as quiet and vague got her sent to me; her boss ordered her to get help with her presentation skills, and fast! To a woman in her late forties well along in her career, this came as a huge blow. In our first session I asked how she had prepared for that fateful meeting with management. She said she did what she always had done. She'd gone over the points that she wished to make in her head and then had "winged it." When I questioned why she hadn't rehearsed aloud, she replied, "Hey, I'm a brilliant winger!" When I inquired how she prepared for more formal presentations, she smiled and said that thankfully she'd been able to avoid them entirely. "Why 'thankfully'?" I asked. Her answer: "Because I'm way too insecure to ever stand in front of a large group and make a formal presentation."

How can a person describe herself as a "brilliant winger" one moment and swear she's insecure the next? Why would someone be frightened of a critique, flying into a rage when his or her skills are questioned, or not only refuse to enter a beneficial learning experience, but attempt to avoid all constructive criticism even in a totally private environment? How can people who appear extremely confident, almost to the point of invincibility, in actuality be so deeply insecure?

Again, confidence and self-esteem are not interchangeable. However, all three (George, Lewis, and Caroline) exhibit what appears to be extremely high self-esteem; "I'm a brilliant winger"; "I don't need help"; "Just show me and I'll get it." In actuality this behavior camouflages their lack of any real self-esteem. This need to camouflage, whether conscious or unconscious, can be highly debilitating, even more debilitating than Janet's low self-esteem. It takes tremendous emotional effort to keep up a bluff. Psychologist Susanne Schad-Somers (in conversation) described both extremes as "'the grandiose and shittiose selves' with neither based in reality." George, Lewis, Caroline, and Janet are perfect examples of this syndrome; their egos are held together with spit and glue. One hint of criticism, and they crumble. They ride the roller coaster between grandiosity and "shittiosity" with a vengeance.

While there are as many variables as people as to how such a self-construct develops, the following case history, albeit extreme, is as good an example as any.

Jack. From his earliest days Jack had bought into his father's dictum that "if you are a genius you don't need to study and if you are less than a genius you shouldn't bother." The father needed Jack to be the genius he, the father, wasn't, and Jack, who exhibited a talent for the arts, spent most of his early years running around from talent to talent trying to be the genius his father longed for. He was either an actor who sang, a singer who danced, or a dancer who acted. He delighted in bragging that he was self-taught, especially when he found himself competing with others just as talented. When he could not sustain his fantasy of "genius," he simply changed fields. He had no choice. To study and compete meant he wasn't a genius; to be less than a genius meant he was nothing. Everything was either black or white. Gray meant average. Average meant failure. Jack refused to accept being "good enough" or to stick it out long enough to acquire tangible skills. Because of this, he always felt insecure, yet he raged at the world for not recognizing him for the genius he was. Eventually the constant seesawing between his "shittiose and grandiose" selves wore him down and, no longer able to sustain the facade, he collapsed and, thankfully, sought and received help.

Not all those who have illusions of grandeur are necessarily whistling "Dixie." Many, like George and Lewis, achieve tremendous success, while just as many others end up as could-have-beens or should-have-beens. What holds true for all is the absence of what Daniel Stern (in *The Interpersonal World of the Infant*) calls "the core self." This core self begins to form between two and six months of age. As we've stated previously, quality attunement (the reinforcing interplay between parent and child) and unstinting adoration during this time—and for a number of months thereafter—contributes to the building of healthy self-esteem. After fifteen months of age, as children move from their own personal world into a "social order," good parental reactions that are age appropriate to the child—such as a curb on grandiose behavior, the reinforcement and praise of actual accomplishments, and, where warranted, nonbelittling reprimands—must occur if the child is to develop properly. Praise not based on actual achievement disables the child and fosters, if not a grandiose personality certainly grandiose behavior. It makes no difference whether or not the parent's need to praise stems from the parent's—or for that matter a teacher's—transferred dreams (Jack's father, the perennial stage parent), or a parent's laziness (easier to spoil or heap false praise onto a child than exert the energy necessary to develop secure accomplished adults), or the parent's own feelings of insecurity. The discrepancy between the overpraised child and how others see the child eventually becomes very shameful. Remember the young man whose father had urged him to recite, and the shame (and its aftermath) he experienced when the young man discovered that no one else had appreciated his performances.

Indiscriminate, false praise and/or holding out of unattainable goals produce fragile egos, which cannot withstand criticism of any kind. Some very wise high school students stated it most succinctly (as quoted by their teacher in a letter to the *New York Times*): "Unrealistic expectations and false praise create . . . obnoxious, self-centered, ego problem classmates" who need to be more than they are or better than everyone else.

Which is not to say that all insecurity is rooted in low self-esteem or, for that matter, grandiosity. Even the most secure among us feel insecure when something threatens our well-being. Remove a support structure: a loved one, job, a home—or even the cast from a healed broken leg—place us in an untenable situation, ask us to perform a task for which we are ill equipped, and depending on how cohesive an inner self we possess and how severe or life-threatening the loss or situation, to varying degrees, we will all suffer feelings of insecurity.

In other words, do not assume that if you become anxious or nervous when you are called upon to make a presentation, speak in public, or present yourself in an unknown situation, you are a grandiose personality. It would be unrealistic to expect anyone to approach a situation—one on which job, position, salary, and future may depend—and not become somewhat concerned. However, if you have prepared yourself adequately and are still nervous, more than likely, part of your nervousness stems from more than a smidgeon of grandiose thinking.

It goes like this:

1) Expect nothing of yourself; you cannot fail.
2) Raise the stakes; you raise the possibility of failure.
3) Raise your skills to meet the stakes; you level the playing field.
4) Raise, or have your expectations raised, beyond the realm of reality (the grandiose self), and the sinking sensation in the pit of your stomach will have good reason to exist. More than that, you will likely experience shame at not having met your unrealistic expectations.

Helen. Out of nowhere, Helen, a heavy-duty rehearser who prided herself on knowing her material inside out and with a reputation for being a fabulous presenter, began having mild panic attacks when she was called upon to make new business presentations. Five months pregnant, she first thought the attacks could be due to a hormonal imbalance or to the fact that she wasn't feeling quite as attractive as before.

Describing herself as a "seductive" presenter who "turned on" in front of an audience, she even wondered if, subconsciously, she believed it was inappropriate for a pregnant woman to seduce anyone other than her husband. The attacks worsened. She called for an appointment.

During our first session it became evident that while some or even all of these factors might be involved, there had to be something more going on. First, while raging hormones could have heightened emotions, if it were only the hormones setting her off, they would be doing so in more than this one situation. Second, it's normal for powerful presenters to get turned on by an audience, but they don't rely on their looks to get their content across. We dug further. Out it came: "Everyone expects me to be so fabulous," she said. "What if I can't pull it off?" There it was. Worried that she wouldn't live up to her reputation, she had begun going for results rather than concentrating on the here and now. In other words, she had been trying to reproduce her last performance without going through the process that had made that performance come alive: transmitting information one bite at a time. Athletes, artists, writers, and scientists will readily verify that going for results produces empty, uninspired, bland performances. It induces anxiety. And, it is an invitation to failure. If you concentrate only on winning approval, you prevent yourself from enacting the very steps that could give you the approval you so desire.

The higher our expectations, the higher our anxiety levels. Like many other women who had actively pursued a career and now, for the first time, were about to experience motherhood, Helen had many mixed emotions. The more she looked forward to the baby's arrival, the more anxious she became as she knew she no longer would be calling the shots. It struck me that she probably had transferred her anxiety over her impending loss of control in her personal life to her work. (Safer to worry about what one can control than about what one can't control.) And worry she did. The more she worried, the more anxious she became.

I explained to Helen that no matter what had gone on before, *fabulous* was a relative term. If she would settle for *good enough,* she would be more than adequate. It took a while, but as this concept began to sink in, I could actually see her relief. With her planned three-month leave of absence pending, I reminded her that once the baby was in the picture, she'd most likely miss a number of presentations, and it might be helpful for others to step in while she was still there to train them. I gingerly mentioned that none of us is indispensable. Slowly, we leveled her expectations to a more realistic level.

We did, however, still have to deal with the impending panic attack, which I had no doubt would occur, because her fear of having one would unconsciously set one off.

Physical Causes of Panic/Anxiety Symptoms

When our brain receives a message of danger—it could be verbal, visual, aural, sensorial—the hypothalamus gland immediately activates the adrenal glands, sending adrenaline and noradrenaline surging through our body. Our blood glucose level rises, our metabolic rate increases, blood vessels in the intestines constrict, those in the muscles dilate, and our eyes widen. Because the original message we received bypassed the cognitive portion of our brain, the adrenaline continues surging through our system before we have had time to ascertain whether or not we need to be afraid, and its effects can continue to be felt even after the real or perceived danger has passed—effects such as the palpitations, sweats, and shaking we can experience after a near-miss car collision.

I armed Helen with an exercise that converts nervousness into positive energy. For many years I, too, had suffered from disabling anxiety attacks and had searched for ways to counter my wobbly legs, tumultuous stomach, hot flashes, and quivering voice, which would overtake me whenever I was called upon to speak extemporaneously. My experience told me that there was no way to wish nerves away or talk myself out of them. Anytime I had tried to "stifle" them, as Archie Bunker would say, my attempt to suppress my nerves only seemed to increase their potency—similar to what happens when you try to suppress a cough. You don't do away with the problem; it keeps growing until those around you wish you'd let out one big honk or croak.

I had tried, unsuccessfully, the "Sarnoff Squeeze"— Dorothy Sarnoff's technique as described in her book *Never Be Nervous Again,* involving the contraction and release of the rectus abdominis muscle, in which you sit erect, hands together in front of you, elbows apart, fingers pointing to the ceiling, and press the palms together while letting out a quiet "sssss" through your teeth. Unsuccessful, because my nerves attacked without warning—even in the middle of a talk that seemed to be going well. Although I believed that Sarnoff's theory had validity, I felt that it just didn't go far enough. It didn't take into consideration all the situations in which presenters could find themselves, or the variety of ways adrenaline acts upon different people. I wanted to create an exercise that could be done at any time, any place, standing, sitting, hands apart, hands together, silently waiting to speak or while in the midst of speaking—one that could be performed without anyone knowing what was taking place. Ergo, the following. Try it!

Exercise to Combat Nervousness

By controlling the muscles of the body, you can begin to control the adrenaline rush and convert it into usable energy.

1) Sit in front of a mirror. Keep your hands relaxed on your knees, your toes relaxed in your shoes.
2) Now, squeeze all the muscles in your body from the collar bone down except for your hands, toes, and those muscles you breathe with, including the stomach. (If you know that you experience nervousness in that pit in your stomach, practice tightening your stomach muscles, but make certain you continue to breathe.)

3) Hold for five seconds and then relax the muscles slowly. Repeat. Keep breathing throughout the exercise even when you're squeezing. Be sure that you cannot see either the tightening or the relaxation in process. If you can't see your muscles move in the mirror, no one else will either.

Variations: Once you've mastered the exercise sitting, try it standing.

Try tightening and relaxing a few muscles at a time.

See if you can talk while tightening and relaxing the basic muscles.

Try carrying on a conversation tightening only selected muscles.

Your face should remain animated; no staring. The last thing you wish to do is look as if you are on the potty. Also, learn to stay with the situation; do not mentally withdraw from the room.

PRACTICE THIS WHEN YOU'RE NOT NERVOUS SO YOU'LL BE ABLE TO USE IT WHEN YOU ARE!

Practice this exercise in meetings, over breakfast, dinner, on the train, walking down the street. Remember: At the first signs of nervousness, don't panic, and don't try to suppress those nerves. Butterflies simply show that you're alive and well with energy to harness. Therefore, at the first signs of nervousness, start squeezing!

Helen practiced the technique for days until she knew she could call on it when and if needed. As I expected, she did experience one last panic attack, but it occurred at home while she rehearsed for her last presentation before she took her leave of absence. When I asked her later what she thought had set it off, she said that she had allowed the importance of this presentation to creep into her thinking. She got over it and went back to rehearsing. At the presentation itself, she focused totally on getting each thought across to her audience. Without a trace of anxiety, she gave a performance equal to what she had always given.

Audiences are not sympathetic to speakers who crave sympathy. There are those who believe that a nervous speaker elicits concern from an audience. While that can happen, concern quickly turns to discomfort. In the process, content gets lost. Audiences cannot worry about whether the speaker is going to survive and simultaneously hear what the speaker has to say. To prove this, I deliberately set a trap for a group of high-profile executives at a seminar. I began by greeting each and every person who entered the room as I always do, introducing myself with a smile, handing out name cards, making everyone as comfortable as possible. Then, after all had taken their seats, in my best posture, best voice, best smile, I began. "There are three elements to a presentation: the presenter, the content, and the audience." A few minutes into my talk I asked the group to play back what I had just said. Not one, I repeat, not one, remembered the first few sentences or had even caught the gist. When I asked why not, they replied, "You appeared nervous." "Was my eye contact good?" I asked. "Oh yes, you looked each of us straight in the eye." "Did my voice sound nervous?" "Oh, no!" "What led you to believe I was nervous?" "You were rubbing your index finger around your thumbnail." That's all it took. That's all it ever takes to distract an audience from your content.

There's no pleasure in watching someone who suffers from sweaty palms, twitching fingers, weak knees—just a few of the signs that reveal nervousness, anxiety, even panic. Audiences, usually being of the captive variety, become easily distressed. Any concern for a speaker's well-being dissipates quickly to embarrassment and then self-pity at being forced to remain in an uncomfortable situation. Even when speakers manage to get their nerves under control, the audience remains poised, antennae up, waiting for another outbreak of nervousness to occur. In turn the speaker, sensing the audience's tension, grows even more nervous. The audience gets more uncomfortable. The speaker becomes more anxious, and on and on it goes, stopping, I'm afraid, with the audience justifiably furious at being placed in an untenable situation. One client, who had doubted this scenario of empathy turning into rage, called me after attending her niece's graduation. "Why, you were right!" she exclaimed. "The main speaker (a well-known author) spoke so softly that she was practically incoherent. It was embarrassing. I couldn't believe it, but it got so bad, I wanted to throttle her."

Speakers who let their own anxieties show, lose their audience's respect, their audience's interest in the subject matter, and the possibility of future interactions.

If your livelihood rests on your presentation of self or presentations in general, it would be unrealistic for you not to worry, but worry itself never changed the course of an event. It only diverts time and energy away from the very activities that can do so. Now fear is something else! I believe in fear. The fear of failure turned one client from a knee-shaking wreck in front of an audience into a Class A speaker. On an upward track at his firm, he knew he could not turn down an invitation to speak to a group of two hundred and fifty potential clients, even though he dreaded speaking in public. Rather than expend his energies on worrying whether or not he'd make an idiot out of himself, he became an obsessive rehearser. Granted, co-workers and family were forced to suffer through one month of madness, a month in which we wrote and rewrote his talk until it sounded like a fireside chat filled with vital information. A month in which he perfected his slides. A month in which he learned physically how to control his knocking knees. A month in which he rehearsed aloud every point he wished to make, and then, when he thought he couldn't repeat it one more time, his fear took over, and repeat he did. Oh, I'm all for fear when it propels us forward.

Therefore, if even thinking about giving a presentation increases your anxiety level; or if, when you do present, these anxieties escalate to such unbearable levels that by the time you open your mouth to speak, nothing comes out—or what does come out emerges in a voice you've never heard before; or if your body tenses, freezing you in place; or you become so jittery that you can't stop moving—GET TO WORK! You already have some exercises to work on. Just keep in mind that we all learn differently. Some people do better concentrating on one skill at a time, others by alternating exercises. Do what works for you. Once again, acquiring a skill takes time. Arnold Palmer didn't perfect his game overnight; Martina Navratilova had to practice, practice, practice; Pavarotti still does scales. You might find the exercise on controlling nervousness a great way to begin, as long as you understand that it does not replace other skills. It only will help ward off the heebie-jeebies until the other skills are in place. Now the really good news:

Controlled adrenaline turns an audience on. Adrenaline not only surges through our bodies when we are in a panic, it also surges through when we are in a state of high anticipation. It just feels different. Those tingling nerve endings or queasy stomach, overbearingly painful when brought on by fear or dread, can be immensely pleasurable when caused by joyful anticipation. Whereas dread causes our pupils to dilate and our skin to tighten, anticipation makes our eyes brighten and our skin glow—qualities that audiences find most appealing. In other words, used correctly, adrenaline can work for you. So don't worry if you get nervous. Just learn to convert that nervousness into excitement.

As to that grandiosity issue: If you believe yourself to be insecure, that is, if you cannot accept constructive criticism without flying into a rage or feeling like a failure, if you need constant praise in order to feel empowered to act, if you feel that you should be exempted from the rules with which most mortals must comply, then perhaps you might consider getting psychological counseling.

If, however, you feel insecure in specific areas, learn what skills you need in order to develop confidence in those areas. If you have made it this far in life, there are enough survival instincts in place not only to help repair whatever damage may have been rendered early on, but to go much further. I am not saying that by learning to comport yourself with ease, you will change your life or repair internal damage, only that achievements, small or large, can enhance one's sense of self.

To come full circle, until you have internalized whatever skills you wish to acquire, you may wish temporarily to fake an air of confidence. I'm quite serious. As long as you do not wing it, but work at mastering whatever skills you require, your pretending you know what you're doing while you are learning to do it can put your audience at ease and help the learning process. Your own ease will come with practice and experience.

CHAPTER 5

Misconception: "Everyone can see what I'm feeling."

One of the most important aspects of effective presentation of self is *cohesion,* the fusing together of our feelings, facial expressions, body language, and content in order that the message we send to others is the one they receive. We have all witnessed the speaker who opens a talk with "Good afternoon. I'm very happy to be here," while looking like someone facing the electric chair, or the TV newscaster with a grin plastered on his face while reporting a grizzly murder. For vastly different reasons, these presenters have disassociated themselves from what they are saying. The speaker, panicked, recites a memorized script without any awareness that she is speaking. The newscaster, playing to the camera, reads words off a Teleprompter without giving thought to what they mean. In *The Interpersonal World of the Infant,* Daniel Stern cites studies that show that "we hear what we see, not what is said." Therefore, no matter how happy the speaker swears she is, we know that she'd prefer a dentist's chair to the podium. As for the newscaster, we can only wonder, as we watch him talk on, whether he enjoys murders, imbibed before the broadcast, or didn't particularly like the victim.

Most likely, both speaker and newscaster would recognize, if it were pointed out to them, that they had disassociated themselves from their material and sent a message other than the one they intended. They are the lucky ones. There are other people who have no awareness of when their disassociation occurs, people who are convinced that they are easy to read—"Why, I'm an open book!"—and are shocked when they learn that the very opposite is true. Here are some examples:

Louise. I was invited to give an after-dinner talk to a group of anesthesiologists. Their profession notwithstanding, it was not to be the most relaxed of evenings. First, the group resembled a delegation from the UN General Assembly, which can be a big problem when your topic is presentation skills and it is apparent that English is not the first language of the majority of your audience. Second, I soon realized that most of the audience had no idea why I had been invited to speak or why they were being required to listen. Third, and definitely the proverbial straw that broke the camel's back, the layout of the room was one of the hardest a speaker can face: an extremely long, narrow room, filled end to end by a long narrow table, with the only decent light hanging over a stationary podium placed in a niche cut out of the center of the longest wall—and no lapel mike available. The reason this is so difficult is that if you, the speaker, turn to look at one side of the room, the people seated on the other side lose sight of your face and, no matter how well you can project, they also lose the sound of your voice. While a lapel mike would have allowed me to move down to one side and speak to the other, thereby giving the impression of including everyone, the lack of light elsewhere in the room all but required me to remain at the podium—something I detest. In my book, preachers stand behind pulpits and preach at, speakers stand in front of their audience and speak with. Besides, due to my subject matter and the fact that I'm my only visual aid, audiences need to see what I'm doing with my body, an impossibility if I'm covered by a podium.

A firm believer in "If it's wrong, fix it!", I decided to ask everyone to move away from the table, push the table back to the wall, and place their chairs in a semi-circle around the niche. All did so, with the exception of one woman who set her chair catty-corner, facing out toward the audience, within inches of where I stood. Then, in full view of her colleagues, in a manner that clearly said "Go on, prove that you have something to tell us that we don't already know," she sat down, crossed her arms and her legs, and then began kicking her foot restlessly into the air while she sucked in her cheeks and distorted her mouth, the way people do when they are intent on telegraphing disdain. She kept this up for the full forty-five minutes of my talk. Moving away from her would have placed me in darkness; staying put forced me to compete with her for the audience's attention. Because she was

one of the group's only English-is-my-first-language
members, she became for many my negative visual
interpreter. It was forty-five minutes of hell. It was
also a lesson I shall never forget.

The minute my ordeal was over she jumped up,
turned to me and said, "My name's Louise; that was
wonderful!" I was stunned. I think I mumbled,
"Could have fooled me," to which she responded,
"Listen, I have a problem." I swear, I bit my tongue.
"No one here takes me seriously," she said. "I'm sure
it's my Midwest accent." Unable to refrain any longer,
I replied, "No. It's your face!" Under the circumstances, any malice on my part could have been justified; however, in all honesty there was none
intended. "Your facial and body language are in direct
opposition to what you are trying to express," I
explained. "What are others to believe? Your words or
your face?"

This story reiterates what we discussed in chapter
3—that even when you keep an eye on your audience,
you cannot assume you know what your audience is
thinking. It also shows that cohesive presentation of
self must exist whether we're speaking or listening,
and it explains why others may not only not hear what
we say, but might hear something we never said.
Louise, unaware that she sent conflicting messages,
couldn't believe that whatever she felt wasn't written
all over her. Obviously, without a cohesive presentation of self, we unwittingly set off a series of misun-
derstandings that can only build negatively one upon
the other.

Dennis. Dennis also believed that others could

read how he felt, understand the meaning of his words, and know exactly who and what he was by simply looking at him. His favorite expression: "My face gives me away every time." He, like Louise, was shocked to learn otherwise. Dennis's reputation preceded him. "Negative, judgmental, unfriendly and demanding" had been his boss's description. His manner during the first hours of a week-long seminar did nothing to refute it. He walked in without acknowledging my presence, seeming to ignore the fact that I was greeting everyone who entered. When I did manage to get his attention and he accepted my outstretched hand, I received a broad smile that lasted but a few seconds before it quickly disappeared, and his face reverted to deadpan. He chose a seat in the front row, slouched down, crossed his arms, extended his legs way out in front, crossed his ankles, and glowered. Even though his face retained a slightly petulant expression, throughout the morning he surprised me by asking questions about overcoming nervousness and quickly responded to questions addressed to the group.

The next day, during the first of his two one-on-one sessions, I asked how he thought he appeared to others. "Too friendly," he said. "I keep telling my wife that I come across like a marshmallow, which is not the way an executive should." As gently as possible, I told him that the previous day I had found his manner disconcerting at best, and at times even threatening. It was a long time before the look of shock left his face.

In working with Dennis, I uncovered a number of factors that explained this dichotomy. One, he had arrived at his company expecting to be welcomed with open arms, even though his job required him to carry out a task that would not endear him to the other employees. It was his job to set the price structures for the products his group sold, and realistic pricing often made the salespeople's jobs more difficult. If he had thought about it he might have realized that the better he did his job, the less likely he was to be accepted into the fold. Two, like Dot in chapter 3, he took the salesforce's frustrations personally, rather than realizing they were directed at what he did, not who he was. Three, trying to live up to his image of how he believed a business executive should behave, he reacted by playing the "professional" and ended up appearing arrogant, judgmental, and demanding (as further discussed in chapter 8). Four, his speech was filled with phrases such as "you should" rather than "if we do this, we could" or "I want" rather than "do you think you could," thereby provoking others to take offense. Unaware of why he was being rejected, he camouflaged the hurt by acting in an even more off-putting manner (similar to Aleah in chapter 2). Last, although he could flash a strong smile, often his facial expressions were in direct opposition to what he meant to convey.

I have no direct knowledge of either Louise's or Dennis's history; however, we can assume that because both seemed to have inappropriate facial responses, their early childhood mirrors and attunements (see chapter 3) were off. For instance, imagine a child running in smiling, looking to its parent for approval, and the parent, in turn, for whatever reason, verbally agreeing but looking concerned. Perhaps the parent furrows his or her brow and tightens the lips. If this happens enough times, the child may incorporate the concerned look into its own repertoire, even when the child is in a good mood.

There are other reasons people may send distinctly wrong signals. As we saw with the speaker who looks miserable as she says "I'm happy to be here," fear can certainly be one of them.

Judith. Judith came into my workshop ready for a fight. If I said "white," she snapped "black." If another person said "great!" the look in her eyes iced our spirits. It was not an auspicious start to a day with a total of five participants, all strangers to each other, who came expecting to enhance their personal communication skills.

Before we all ran for the hills, I asked Judith whether she was aware she had been attacking us from the moment she entered. She looked at me as if I had lost it. Attacking us? No way! When I repeated—and the group confirmed—that this was what we had experienced, she turned contrite. Suddenly our warrior appeared to be a lost soul. I asked her if she had felt panicked. The others now looked at me as if I were slightly mad, until I explained that belligerence sometimes can be a camouflage, a way of acting out the dictum, either consciously or unconsciously, that the best defense is a good offense. What could be more offensive than a hostile attack? Judith admitted that she had felt panic, but she wasn't aware that she had attacked anyone. There were two aspects of the situation that both Judith and the rest of the group found particularly surprising: one, that what Judith was feeling internally had translated itself into entirely different behavior externally, and two, that the others weren't able to see what she felt.

Judith believed that her panic stemmed from having been warned that I was a hard taskmaster, combined with her fear of presentations in general. Keep in mind that studies show that people are more frightened of public speaking than they are of death, heights, or snakes. This is why I strongly urge companies to offer my workshop only to those who truly want it. It is hard enough to work on your personal and professional communication skills in a public setting! It is harder still to do so against your will. However, even when participants agree to come or decide to do so completely on their own, the anxiety levels can be astounding.

Susan. Susan wasn't sent by anyone. She knew she had a problem with speaking in front of others and decided it was time to deal with it. Her decision did nothing to calm her nerves, however. The workshop took on mythical proportions as the day neared, eventually looming in her mind as her final scene on earth. To make matters worse, the New York transit system snarled on the morning of the workshop, causing her to be late, something that all who attend my workshops are warned against in advance. I realize that there are times when no matter what you do, the gods cause you to be late, but in my book, continual lateness shows a clear disrespect and lack of concern for others as in "My time is more valuable than yours." I'm known for being rather lunatic on the subject and warn clients of that fact by letter and phone before each workshop, which is why I was more than taken aback when Susan arrived twenty minutes late and came sauntering in exuding an air of calm.

We can only imagine what it was like for the already anxiety-ridden Susan. She later confessed that on the way from the subway she had seriously considered turning around and going back home, but the thought that she had already paid kept her walking that last mile to my door. I, expecting her to appear out of breath from trying to be on time or at least to extend an apology, added to her misery by inquiring if she was aware how late she was. She added to mine by responding "Yes," and then proceeded to withdraw to the bathroom to "freshen up," delaying the start of the workshop even more.

Once the workshop began, she showed very little range of expression. The group, to a person, described her as shy. Then late in the morning, during the breathing exercises that concentrate on relaxation (see chapter 7 and the appendix), more than a chink appeared in her armor. Out of nowhere, tears began to flow. Fighting back a cracking voice, she whispered that she'd better leave and return some other day. I urged her to see it through—at least until lunch—explaining to her and the rest of the group that her tears were in fact a release from all the tension that had been building over weeks.

Looking back, I realized that she had given me a signal as to just how scared she was during our first conversation when she hadn't blinked an eye, so to speak, at the cost of the workshop. Not that the cost is out of line, but normally those who are in relatively low-paying fields and plan to pay on their own usually take a moment to think it over, asking if time payments are possible or if they can get a reduced rate. Although I remember momentarily thinking it strange that she did none of the above, for whatever reason I had let it slide—a mistake. If I had it to do again I should have guessed that her stoic acceptance was that of someone who, having made the decision to attend, had steeled herself to coming no matter what, much as someone does who is faced with having to undergo a terrible medical procedure. I should have asked how she felt about coming and talked through her anxieties either in a private session or on the phone. Fortunately Susan not only stayed through the day, participating fully in all the remaining exercises and discussions, but returned for the follow-up sessions.

Whereas Judith fought her discomfort by going on the offensive—like a fearful cat who instinctively puffs its hair, shows its claws, and hisses, Dennis acted the judgmental schoolmaster and Susan turned into an inscrutable wall. Fear can do that. Others may show nothing at all.

Charles. Except for Charles's darting eyes, which never met another soul's, it would have been impossible to tell that he felt anything at all. He appeared to be a person seemingly without affect, someone emotionally cut off from himself and others. Even during those moments when Charles physically exhibited intense emotion—such as when I suggested he get help other than mine, and in a display of great relief he fell against the wall and sank down to the floor—his facial muscles never moved.

Do not assume that Charles was nonfunctioning. In his late forties, he had held a number of very good jobs. He came to me because the firm he worked for was undergoing a restructuring, and Charles, having been fired once before and being afraid it could happen again, wished help with job interviewing skills.

There are people like Charles, who seek my services rather than take the more appropriate step of seeking psychological counseling. Sometimes I can direct them to a therapist immediately; sometimes it takes a bit longer. Depending on what aspects of their presentation they wish to work on, I make the determination as to whether or not to continue with them. Since Charles reacted to my suggestion by setting up an appointment with a therapist, and the therapist believed it was important that he continue with me as well, I tackled his outside persona, while the therapist went to work repairing the internal damage.

Charles's lack of expression was couched in his past, which, as he later shared, had been filled with alternating periods of verbal abuse and neglect. The abuse, his age, his appropriate panic at what he was facing in the business community, as well as years of personal problems that had been swept under the rug, were not problems that could be healed or dealt with overnight. It required enormous time and energy on everyone's part. While I attempted to improve his lack of affect display and to help him focus his darting eyes, those particular aspects of our work together would not and could not be resolved until a great deal of the internal reparative work was in place.

What should by now be obvious is that we make an enormous mistake when we assume that we can correctly interpret body language. While Charles actually suffered from lack of affect (the apparent inability to show emotions), Jim, the young man from chapter 3, was simply self-conscious about his good looks. I also had a client who didn't move his facial muscles because he didn't wish to activate a painful nerve in his cheek—the result of an automobile crash. I had another who kept her face immobilized because her parents—who valued looks over brains—repeatedly stressed that her face was beautiful when in repose. Then there was the man who did not want to resemble his highly histrionic parent whom he found embarrassing. Whatever the reason for poor facial or body language—be it emotional or physical impairment, vanity, poor or inappropriate early childhood mirroring, or rebellion—poor nonverbal language results in off-putting, negative, and misleading presentation of self; it also reflects negatively on your message.

An audience will always believe your expression over your words. More than that, your mood as reflected on your face will change your audience's reactions to your material. As discussed in the introduction, our moods color our responses. If we're in an upbeat mood upon entering a movie theater, we might react to a bad movie with amusement; if we enter in a bad mood, unless we go truly wanting to change our mood, a really good movie may leave us cold.

If we wish to affect others, our bridge is our

affect display—our ability visibly to reflect the emotions we wish to express. To warm an audience to one's ideas or product, it's mandatory to make the audience receptive, and no amount of positive adjectives—such as *great, wonderful, fabulous, memorable*—can ever counter a face that looks inert, blank, concerned, or worried. Adjectives are grammatically required to describe accurately the noun they modify. The black car. The tall, iced, minted drink. The soup-to-nuts computer manual. Adjectives such as *fantastic, tremendous, exciting,* and *memorable,* do not add to the description. All they tell us is that the presenter who uses them is lazy or is unable to describe concretely an idea or product. People who sell with these adjectives inadvertently bring the unscrupulous used car salesmen to mind. Audiences rightly assume that lazy adjectives are meant to cover for lack of substance, but an audience does not interpret vocal and visual effects such as sounds, facial expressions, or hand and body movements as lazy.

To illustrate how necessary strong visual and vocal effects are and how unnecessary adjectives can be, I often stand in front of an audience and tell them about the dessert I had the night before—a fantastic piece of apple pie chock-full of tart apples and white raisins, loaded with cinnamon and made with an extraordinarily crisp thin crust. Then, I follow with version two: "I had a piece of pie last night." You, the reader, might have salivated over the first piece of pie, but it is this last piece audiences always want—but then you are not watching me recount the ingredients in a flat voice with no expression on my face whatsoever, or seeing me deliver the second version in a state of ecstatic delight followed by a sigh that contains a slightly orgasmic remembrance of the evening past. While it may appear that my audiences are simply responding to my "performance," the actual sequence of events is slightly more complicated. First, we often, unconsciously, mimic another person's facial expression, which means that if we're smiled at, we most likely will smile back. Second, as we will see a bit later in the chapter, our facial expressions can change our mood; therefore, if we are made to smile, our mood will elevate. Third, moods are infectious, which is why my audiences usually fall in with my mood, and once they are in a better mood, they then become more receptive to what I'm "selling."

Before you continue with this chapter, get a small hand mirror and keep it handy. Now, stop for a moment and think of something that you truly enjoy, something that makes you feel good inside. Don't edit your thoughts. Even if someone is in the room with you, they cannot read your mind. When your feelings take hold, look into the mirror. Does your face reflect your feelings? Could a stranger read your mood? Try it again, but this time think of something that annoys you—perhaps that neighbor who plays music too loud or the car alarm that goes off at 6 A.M. Sunday mornings. When you feel truly irked, look again. Has your face changed sufficiently so that the stranger can once again see your mood? If true pleasure and annoyance showed on your face, you can feel confident that you do not lack affect. If they didn't, you may not have felt the depth of pleasure or annoyance that one needs for affect. Try this again with other images. If your face still does not respond correctly, try moving your facial muscles until they do respond appropriately, such as a small smile for a small pleasure, a tight jaw and squinty eyes for annoyance.

Under no circumstances do I wish you to fake emotions; there is nothing worse than a phony—but real feelings that light up a face do transmit to others. Nor do I advocate wearing your feelings on your sleeve. There are times when a poker face comes in quite handy. Still, our face is our most important visual aid. It is where others look to see if we're telling the truth, where they check to see if we believe what we're saying, where they find out if we're not only listening, but agreeing (or not) with what is being said. If you can control your facial messages, the message you wish to send will be the one others receive.

Again, this is a book on presentation skills. To present effectively, we need energy and passion—passion for our subject, and energy so that our passion transmits to others. For some of you, passion may seem too large a concept; therefore, feel free to substitute relish. Technicians can relish new technological advances. A number-crunching analyst can do the same.

Do not think that because others may view your subject as passionless, that you are allowed to appear passionless about your subject. (Great actors are said to be able to read the phone book and bring an audience to tears.)

Not all of us have the luxury of presenting information about which we're passionate or even mildly enthused. What if on the day of a presentation you feel out of sorts, or you've had a fight with your spouse, friend, or landlord, been elbowed in the subway, or had your car totaled by an uninsured driver? What if you are simply overtired and running low on energy? What do you do to project sincere enthusiasm? Bad moods are not easily dissipated. We tend to luxuriate in snits and resist anyone who tries to pull us out. "Don't talk to me," we say. "Let me wallow alone." While time and change of circumstance normally combine to extricate us from negative thoughts, usually we don't have the time or the ability to change our circumstance. When time is of the essence, we need first to attack the problem physically, before we attack it mentally.

As I stated earlier, facial expressions can change our mood, at least according to Paul Ekman and Richard Davidson, who have pinpointed a specific facial muscular contraction that elevates mood. They dubbed it the Duchenne marker, for Benjamin Amand Duchenne who, in the 1880s, not only mapped out the movements of a hundred facial muscles, but recognized that "'frank joy is expressed on the face by the combined contraction of the zygomatic major muscle and the orbicularis oculi.'" The study concluded that the contraction of the outer portion of the orbicularis oculi muscle (which surrounds the eye) and the zygomatic major muscle (which runs from the cheekbone to the outer side of the lip) stimulates the portion of the brain that induces joy. They also discovered that smiles that only use the zygomatic major muscle can camouflage other moods; they express or reflect joy, but will not induce it. In an earlier study Ekman and his colleagues found that most of us can voluntarily contract the inner part of the eye muscle—evident in a tightened and raised lower eyelid—but few can voluntarily contract the outer portion that raises the cheeks, producing crow's feet wrinkles. That does not mean that those of you who can't are doomed to joyless lives. It simply means that you will have to learn how to find the muscle and contract it. It can take a bit of work, but as with any muscle in the body, work usually produces results.

Exercise:

1) Pick up the mirror and search for the indicated muscle. If you cannot contract it, grin from ear to ear until you find yourself squinting the outer portion of the eye muscle.
2) Keeping the eye muscle squinted, slowly allow the grin to leave the rest of your face. If the eye muscle drops, try again. Repeat until you are able to maintain the squinted muscle without the grin. Once you've achieved this, you have activated the muscle. From this point on it is simply a matter of practice until you can squint on command.

If we are already in a decent mood, the stimulation derived from this exercise may give us most of the energy we need. However, in a miserable mood, it will likely only bring us up to neutral, and for a presenter, neutrality is insufficient. To generate within us the passion needed to energize an audience, we will have to put our brains to work.

EXERCISE:

STEP ONE: Close your eyes and think about someone you love or something you love to do. It could be your favorite food—strawberries do it for one of my clients—a trip you took, making a hole in one, or, of course, sex. Don't worry; even if someone is in the room with you, none of us can read minds, so enjoy your thoughts.

If you need something with a bit more bite—and I fully admit to being someone who does—imagine that you have finally wreaked revenge on someone who has been a thorn in your side. Again, it makes no difference what you think about as long as eventually you're energized. When you feel thoroughly turned on, open your eyes and look in the mirror.

Again, do not become concerned if the turn-on you've chosen doesn't show on your face. Often what we assume lights our fire may not produce the desired visual result. For instance, if forbidden fruits are your fantasy, you may have learned how to keep your face immobile while you are fantasizing, so as not to be discovered, and it will be hard to break this habit. You also need to search for a turn-on that will consistently work for you. Thinking about someone you care deeply about can produce many diverse feelings, too diverse to work as a fire starter. Thinking about a cherished pet can also be problematic because 1) it can make you feel warm rather than energized, and 2) if the pet gets ill, you will not be able to rely on your turn-on. You wish to find something that can be used under any circumstances. Finding it may take a bit of searching. I've had clients go through a roster of categories until they come upon their specific turn-on. When you find your particular turn-on, you should feel a small wave of electricity pulsate through your veins.

Check again to be certain that your expression reflects how you feel. Study your face in the mirror. Are your eyes aglow? Do the outer corners crinkle? Do the corners of your mouth turn upward? Are your eyebrows unfurrowed? Could that stranger recognize how good you feel and be infected by it? Keep trying until you visibly feel and see what you wish to transmit.

STEP TWO: Maintain your good feeling and, looking in the mirror, say, "I hate champagne." You may wish to turn on a tape recorder so that you can play back how you sound.

The mirror should reflect back an image of someone who relishes disliking champagne. (The tape, if you have one, should do the same.) This is not to turn you into one of those presenters who comes across like a thousand-watt bulb in a tiny closet, that is, a person whose outward display of emotion is clearly false, overly stated, and inappropriate to the situation. If you give an audience a real emotion, let them know you feel it, and let them see it, you can omit an extraordinary amount of words. For instance, the speaker mentioned in the beginning of this chapter would only have had to say "Hi," and if she appeared happy, everyone would have known she was very happy to be there.

CHAPTER 6

Misconception: "My work speaks for itself."

A few years back, I met with a creative director of an advertising agency to discuss training his staff to become more effective presenters. In the course of our discussion I used the words to sell, as in "showing your people how *to sell* their ads rather than merely presenting them." "I don't want them selling!" he bristled. "I want them persuading. We're not used car salesmen, you know. We're creatives!"

At the time, his response struck me as rather comical, considering that his job was to create advertising, as well as to supervise others in the creation of advertising designed to *sell* his clients' products. He reminded me of a single person who goes to a singles' event and swears he doesn't want to meet anyone. With the creative director's assistant in the room, I refrained from semantic war games; back at the studio, I headed straight for the dictionary.

Not one pejorative tinge could I find in my 1967 *Unabridged Random House*'s definitions of the verb *to sell*: 1. "to give up or make over to another for a consideration; dispose of to a purchaser for a price"; 2. "to deal in; keep or offer for sale"; 3. "to make a sale"; and what I certainly would have used had I decided to do semantic battle: 4. "to persuade or induce (someone) to buy something."

Because dictionaries can vary widely, and I did not wish to short change the creative director, I switched to the *Oxford English Dictionary*. Its first definition of *sell*, which seems actually to have been the very first definition, was positive: "a seat, or low stool; a seat of dignity." My satisfaction was short-lived. From that point on our mother tongue's obsolete definitions certainly placed closer to the creative director's view of the word than mine: 2. "an act of betraying or giving up to justice. 1838 Dickens's O.Twist xxvi, 'I say . . . what a time this would be for a sell! I've got Phil Barker here; so drunk, that a boy could take him' " followed by "sell out" or "sell your soul to the devil." My mood rallied as it became apparent that somewhere between Dickensian England and present times, the Brits decided that *to sell* simply defined a transaction between two parties, that is, "to give up or hand something over to another for money . . . to vend." I turned to *vend.* Again, "to sell, to dispose of through sale, to trade in as a seller." No implied negative bias; no "persuasion" either. Now, this could have led me to conclude that the English do not believe in persuasion—either subtle or overt—in selling, but I knew that they in particular have a penchant for subtle messages. The English possess an extreme disdain toward American ways and consider our overt sales techniques more than a touch déclassé. Just look how they reacted to a Boboli Bread television commercial created by the London-based office of an American agency. In it a young, friendly chef chats to the camera on how to prepare the bread, while his mother's off-camera voice interrupts. The only real sell line in the entire commercial comes at the end when the young man sweetly explains, "It's more than a pizza. It's a Boboli." American advertising folk, used to more direct "buy, or else!" type pitches, shook their heads in disbelief when, according to Reuters, the Brits rejected the spot because it was "too hard sell, too American."

I left the Brits and decided to check out the 1994 *Electronic English Dictionary*. I found the transitive verb defined as: 1) "to exchange or deliver for money or its equivalent"; 2) "to offer for sale, as for one's business or livelihood"; 3) "to give up or surrender in exchange for a price or reward"; 4) "to be responsible for the sale of; promote successfully"; and, still at the bottom of the list, 5) "to persuade (another) to recognize the worth or desirability of." As for the intransitive verb: 1) "to exchange ownership for money or its equivalent; engage in selling"; 2) "to be sold or be on sale"; and my favorite: 3) "to attract prospective buyers." Just to make certain that I covered all bases, I looked up *persuade*: 1) "to induce or undertake a course of action or embrace a point of view by means of argument, reasoning or entreaty." The synonyms: "induce, prevail, convince," which, dear creative director, means that as of this writing, on both sides of the Atlantic, not one definition of *sell* conjures up unscrupulous used car hustlers and fast-talking foot-in-the door salespeople. And persuasion? It describes a style of selling. At its root still sits that seat of dignity, the *sell!*

It isn't only people who work in nonquantifiable fields such as interior design, consulting, public relations, and the like—fields in which benefits cannot be measured in concrete terms—who share the creative director's conflicted attitudes toward selling. On one level they accept that inanimate objects cannot speak for themselves, that clients often need to be persuaded, and that all of us can improve the manner in which we present. On a much deeper level, however, there remains the suspicion that if something needs to be sold, it must be defective. (Aren't all used cars really lemons?) It is this suspicion, what we could call the misconception behind the misconception, that inhibits even those who have quantifiable results and/or products to "sell" their wares. Recently, I witnessed an example of this behavior when I stopped at a cosmetic counter that features the line of makeup I normally use. Needing a lift, I asked the saleswoman if she thought I should buy a different foundation. She responded with "What do you want?" I told her I didn't know what I wanted; what would she suggest? She said it depended on what I was looking for. I said I didn't know what I was looking for, and if I did, I wouldn't be asking her opinion. She said that it had nothing to do with her opinion, because it depended on the look I was going for. I repeated that if I knew the look to go for, I would simply ask for the product that would give me that look. She remained adamant. Fascinated as to how long this could go on, I continued until my time ran out and I had to leave— needless to say, empty-handed. If all she was doing was trying to adhere to the salesperson's dictum "Give the customer what the customer wants," then she hadn't listened to what I wanted. I had wanted to feel different, to be momentarily pampered, and, most important, to be sold. Most likely she assumed that her products would sell not only because they existed, but because value wins out every time. Of course, if that were true, then more than two of van Gogh's paintings would have sold in his lifetime.

Value does not always win out. Without getting into a discussion of what makes something valuable within a culture, much of what we now accept as having value was first promoted, that is, promoted in order for us to perceive the value. Within a decade, computers went from those machines that few of us would ever use to being almost as commonplace as telephones. They did so not simply because they became more affordable and user friendly, but because of word of mouth, marketing, and a great deal of public relations and advertising that told us why we should want them in our homes and offices. Drug companies employ door-to-door salespeople (probably the only people left in the medical community, other than ambulance attendants, to make house calls) who go from doctor to doctor touting the latest drug, proclaiming its worth in order to convince doctors to prescribe it to their patients. Does this mean that all those in sales, advertising, marketing, and public relations mean to sell us a bill of goods? In some cases, yes; most of the time, no. Most people believe in what they espouse, but they also understand that the majority of us are more comfortable looking at something with a seal of validation stamped upon it. There's nothing wrong with doing so. The people who created the Good Housekeeping Seal—originally called the Seal of Approval—understood a consumer's need for such validation. Their concept: to assure the consumer that all products which carry the seal were as advertised in the magazine. The seal still assures Good Housekeeping's readers a high level of quality. I for one would much prefer to "buy" something or someone that has been tested, comes highly recommended, and sports viable credentials. If this shows a lack of derring-do on my part, so be it.

While a validation, or sell, does not guarantee acceptance, it does not imply that a work, product, idea, or person lacks quality or substance. A sell only predisposes a consumer, in our case an audience, to consider the work, product, idea, or person being offered. Of course, the more passionately the seller advocates the product, the more consideration the audience may give it.

Advocacy!—now there's a word that, although not found in the lexicons with respect to *sell,* in my opinion, it should be. To advocate, is what we do—or should do—when we present or sell. We speak *for* something. Of course, to speak for implies there's someone to speak to, and, as there's nothing that turns an audience off quicker than being spoken to, or at, if we wish to be effective advocates, we will need to learn how to speak with. Time and again I watch charming conversationalists lose the "with" when they get up to present. They become automatons, or worse, lecturers. It's not easy to speak with. Certainly it requires a conversational style of presentation; it also involves strategy.

Strategy

One last definition: *Random House* describes strategy as: 1. "generalship; the science or art of combining and employing the means of war in planning and directing large military movements and operations"; 2. "the use of an instance of using this science or art"; 3. "skillful use of a stratagem" ("*Stratagem: a plan, scheme or trick to surprise an enemy*"); and last, 4. "a plan, method, or series of maneuvers or stratagems for obtaining a specific goal or result."

Just as facial affect builds an emotional bridge between you and your audience (see chapter 5), a well-developed strategy constructs an intellectual one. It insures that what you present—be it yourself, information, or a product—gets delivered. As we shall see, without a strategy, a presentation stays on the presenter's side of the road, leaving the audience unable to connect to what is being presented. I used a strategy to develop this book. The steps are as follows:

1) **I pinpointed my audience.** I ascertained that my audience would be past, present, and future clients, as well as those who were unable to work directly

with me due to distance or circumstance—in other words: you.

2) **I determined your possible motivations.** What I call the "carrots"—the incentives that when dangled in front of us, motivate us to act. I decided that your carrots were: personal advancement, the elimination of the distress and discomfort experienced when you present yourself and your ideas to others, and the promise of a confident self.

3) **I defined my "to do."** A "to do" is whatever a presenter wants his or her audience to do *after* the presentation concludes. My "to do" was for you to develop your skills on a daily basis and to eradicate wishful thinking.

4) **I developed a strategy.** Because all successful strategies must include the audience's "carrots" and the presenter's "to do," my strategy was to find ways to prove to you that you could achieve all of your carrots by developing your skills, giving you example after example of how the process works and of the thinking behind it.

5) **I created a theme.** A theme should emerge directly from the strategy. It can be the strategy itself; it can camouflage the strategy; it can be an extension of the strategy. Because experience had taught me that to make my strategy viable, I had to eradicate those misconceptions or learning blocks that client after client had voiced. My theme became: how to overcome the misconceptions that inhibit us.

Other Examples of the Process

Example 1. The Presenter: *Rosemary,* a director of an organization that raises money to exhibit, for view and sale, the work of physically and emotionally disabled artists.

The audience: A community association.

The audience's request: For Rosemary to speak about her organization at a luncheon.

The task as presented to me: Rosemary wanted to develop a more dynamic personal style of presentation.

Rosemary's original presentation: Rosemary had filled her speech with detailed information about her organization, how it started, its mission, where the next series of events would take place, and so on. It lacked audience relevance. In order to construct a bridge, we formulated a "to do."

Her audience's carrots: Getting Rosemary to list her audience's carrots was no easy task. First, her own reasons for speaking kept intruding on the objectivity she needed to analyze her audience. Second, she doubted that she could decipher the individual carrots of an audience made up of fifty to seventy-five different people. The truth is that no one can, but you can compile a list of general carrots. Eventually, Rosemary's audience carrot list read:

1) A desire to be involved in community activities (whether to occupy time or to fulfill an altruistic need).
2) Ego gratification through recognition of good deeds, whether involving money or time.

3) An interest in the arts.
4) A need to expand personal contacts.

While undoubtedly others existed, these were sufficient to formulate a strategy.

Her "to do": I rejected Rosemary's first "to do," which was to have her audience ask questions about the organization. It did not stimulate true involvement. I accepted "to get my audience to offer time and money to the organization—if that's not realistic, time *or* money will suffice." This "to do" was honest, direct, and involving.

Rosemary's strategy: We combined Rosemary's audience's "carrots" with her "to do" and developed the strategy: "to show how personal involvement with the organization—whether by donating time, money or both—the audience would expand its circle of friends, receive ego gratification, and do it all while enjoying the visual arts." Because Rosemary had to break down any fears her audience might have about becoming involved with disabled artists, we decided she would talk about specific artists and the personal benefits she herself had derived, making a point to discuss specifically those benefits that directly corresponded to her audience's carrots.

Rosemary's theme: The artists themselves and the rewards of knowing them.

The results: Rosemary's speech went over so well that she continues to be asked to speak throughout the state. She has increased community involvement and has received additional financing. More importantly, she has developed a confidence in her presentation style that she describes as having grown because of her newfound ability to attach herself to her audience.

The more you know about your audience, the better the chance you have to connect. We cannot always know what may motivate an audience. There are times when more than a bit of Holmesian sleuthing is needed to uncover what those carrots might be. For instance, instead of selling you on presentation skills, let's say that I sell vacuum cleaners. I call on you, but you've just purchased one. On the surface it appears that there would be no way to reach you, but I sleuthed. I discovered that you have allergies. Your carrot: anything that reduces dust in your apartment. As it happens, my vacuum has a far better system of containing dust than the one you bought. Voilà! A sale.

The more time you take researching your audience's carrots, the stronger bridge you will build between your audience and yourself. When you're not certain what those carrots may be, make assumptions. Perhaps your audience needs more business contacts, a better bottom line, increased productivity, recognition, money, advancement, or ego gratification. I could just as easily have called on someone who doesn't suffer from allergies, but who must own the very latest product on the market.

A "to do" may need to be invented.

EXAMPLE 2. The Presenter: *Karl,* the manager of a test farm for a company that develops agricultural products.

The audience: All new employees.

The audience's request: In this case, management's request: that Karl improve the tour of the farm that all new employees must take.

The task as presented to me: Karl explained that he'd been told his tours were dull, that he didn't feel he communicated well, and that he was uncomfortable in the role of tour guide.

Karl's original presentation: The obvious: a running commentary about how the farm worked.

His audience's carrots: All new employees want speedy integration into their new environment. We decided this would be the overriding motivator.

Karl's "to do": Karl had no "to do" when he started; in fact he swore there was none. Then, as he thought about it, he realized that he could invent one that would relate to his audience's motivator. He became incredibly creative. He decided that he wanted those on the tour to plant a garden.

His strategy: To show the new employees that by planting a garden (whether it be in a pot in the kitchen or a plot of land outside their house), they would be better able to understand the company culture, have reasons to call on different people for advice, and thereby expand their circle and become integral to the organization.

Karl's theme: Grow a garden and belong.

The results: Whether or not those who took the tour ever grew a garden, Karl's tour took on an exciting aura. Because he was passionate about farming, he was able to communicate his passion to others, to engage his audience while showing them all the facets of the farm.

The same way a "to do" may not be obvious, neither may be a strategy.

Example 3. The Presenter: *Ron,* a consultant for an accounting firm.

The audience: His firm's client, a nationwide trucking company.

The audience's request: For Ron to teach a new software program to the trucking company's systems department.

The task as presented to me: Ron wanted to teach the program in such a way so that no one would call him with questions later. Although I believe that a teacher should teach so that students learn, I questioned why a consultant would want to suspend contact with clients. He was adamant. He did not want his clients to call him with questions after he had taught them the program.

Ron's original presentation: A stern walk through the program.

His audience's carrots: Fear! All had heard there would be a downsizing—that euphemistic term for layoffs—and all were frightened they could lose their jobs.

His "to do": In this case, a "not to do." No calls!

Ron's strategy: Over time I've asked many clients to analyze Ron's particular situation and come up with a strategy Ron could have used. The majority responded exactly as Ron had, with strategies such as telling students that they could lose their jobs if they didn't learn the program, or that they would have a better chance to keep their job if they did. Statements such as these only reinforce an audience's fear, and **fear inhibits learning**. Once Ron understood this psychological component of learning, he decided to teach with analogies, that is, to find parts of other programs that his audience already knew and show how similar they were to what he was now teaching. He also developed some games, assigned one person for each part of the program to become the "expert," and created a series of tests to be taken at each stage of the program. It took a bit longer, but this reduced his audience's fears, allowed them to take in the information, and accomplished his "to do."

Ron's theme: You already know this.

The result: His clients learned the program. I did, however, suggest that Ron follow up with phone calls to see how each participant was faring. He could do so at his own convenience and therefore control the flow of calls and still stay in touch with clients. It never hurts.

As stated in the introduction, we all view the world through our own personal history. Preconceived ideas, education, mood of the moment, expectations, and needs all play into how we hear, see, understand. While we all have had moments when we've read another's thoughts correctly, those incidents are rare and often either coincidental or result from years of togetherness. No one ever sees exactly what we see, hears exactly what we hear, understands exactly what we understand. Our past and present realities are ours alone. Not even our closest intimates will ever experience an event in the precise manner that we experience it. If you doubt this, ask a group of friends or colleagues to say the first word that comes to mind when you say "milk," and make note of the wide range of responses you get—from coffee to cow to chocolate to lactose intolerance. Now, if a common word can call up such a variety of associations to friends and colleagues, imagine the vast array of interpretations being made by people we don't know as well.

Audiences cannot read between our lines.

Example 4. The Presenter: *Andrew,* a portfolio manager.

The audience: Five board members of a pension fund and their consultant.

The audience's request: For the portfolio manager and the senior vice president in charge of marketing to show why the board should hire them to manage a portion of the pension fund's assets. The normal protocol for these presentations is that the marketer gives an overview of the firm and its resources, after which the portfolio manager explains the rationale behind the process of managing the portfolio.

The task as presented to me: The marketer requested that I "do something" with the portfolio manager's style, which was "esoteric" and "deadly."

While each firm works in its own unique way, marketers of funds are usually the first contact the client meets, the portfolio manager arriving for the "finals." While the marketer will have touted the fund's performance, the impression the portfolio manager makes on the board will determine whether or not an investment of capital is to be made. Because presentations are often strictly timed with very little chance of one-on-one interactions, the portfolio manager has to convey credibility, trustworthiness, and savvy in but a few moments. Although I am never comfortable with generalizations, most marketers enjoy the selling process, while portfolio managers prefer to research companies and trade stocks. For them, having to make a presentation holds the same attraction as undergoing a root canal, and I have no doubt that some, given the option, would much prefer the dentist chair. In the old days, they could stay glued to the trading desk. Today, due to the nature of the business and the proliferation of money managing firms from which pension boards now can choose, portfolio managers have no choice but to venture out into the world to help retain clients and win new ones.

Andrew's original presentation: A recitation of facts and figures. Andrew fell into the category of presenters who drone on and on, assuming that truth alone attracts.

His audience's carrots: Low risk; high returns.

His "to do": To get the board to agree to hire his firm.

Andrew's strategy: The same as his marketer's: to show the board how Andrew's personal strategy of picking stocks has yielded consistent high returns with very low risk, and would continue to do so. As important as it was for Andrew to sell his strategy, it was just as important that he sell himself. He was the person who would be handling the pension board's money.

Andrew's theme: The same as his strategy: You, the board of directors, need low risk and high rewards. I have structured my portfolio to meet that exact criteria. Here's the proof.

The results: By consistently and constantly reiterating the board's goals, Andrew began to speak *with* rather than at his audience, which made him and his message more accessible. Andrew had always assumed that the board would make its own connections between his portfolio's performance and the pension fund's needs, but it wasn't the board's job to build a bridge, any more than it was the board's job to guess Andrew's "to do"—something Andrew also often omitted mentioning. Here, too, he had assumed the audience would get it. Once he started directly asking for what he wanted, he became real to the board members, someone they could relate to, someone to whom they could entrust their money.

Adding a rationale. You ensure a truly effective presentation when you follow each of the steps discussed above. This is true when you present something tangible or when you present what I previously referred to as a nonquantitative product or service. In this last category, however, one additional element needs to be added: the rationale.

Products such as advertising, design, consulting services, and the like often require that audiences not only take a leap of faith concerning the potential benefits of the product, but they often have to imagine what the finished product will actually look like. That's hard when we all view the world within the framework of our own reality. What may be apparent to us, will not necessarily be to someone else. If you, as a presenter, want others to envision exactly what you see in your mind's eye, then you must take them step by step through the thinking process that led you to your conclusions—even if that process was mostly intuitive. I do not want to leave the impression that all things can be presented in a similar manner; they can't. However, although the styles of presenting change, the steps toward developing a connection between the presenter and the audience—the strategy—do not! All the same rules apply.

EXAMPLE 5. The Presenters: *Don and Geraldine.* An architect and an interior designer.

The audience: A hospital board.

The audience's request: For the architect and interior designer to present their plans for the remodeling of a hospital entrance, solarium, and wing.

The task as presented to me: To make certain that their presentation sold the plans. I asked for a list of the audience's carrots, board member by board member.

The carrots: For the financial officer: low costs. For the hospital administrator, with three area hospitals competing for patients: a beautiful interior to attract patients. For the facilities manager: ease of maintenance. For the head doctor and head nurse, who were both in on the decision-making process: less distance to travel within the hospital grounds. All expressed a desire for floor-to-ceiling windows wherever possible in order to bring the outside in.

The "to do": To get the board to agree to the plans.

Don and Geraldine's strategy: To show the board how each of the member's considerations were taken into account and met wherever possible. We also decided that Don and Geraldine should try to meet privately with each board member before the big meeting in order to overcome individual objections, thereby eliminating a free-for-all when the board met as a group.

The inclusion of the rationale. Geraldine and Don soon realized that it was not enough simply to describe the elements and to show how they met the board's needs. They also had to include the thinking that had led to specific choices of materials, color, and architectural decisions. This allowed the board not only to follow along, but to feel more educated and therefore a part of the decision-making process. Imagine what would have happened if they had assumed that the board had understood their decision not to use floor-to-ceiling windows because in order to keep costs down, they didn't want to move the heating elements that ran along the lower portion of all outside walls.

Don and Geraldine both have spent years in their respective fields. In many cases, their decisions were intuitive; therefore, they needed to construct a rationale after the fact so that the board did not feel their decisions were arbitrary. Keep in mind that an audience wishes to feel knowledgeable enough to make a decision, and in order to do so, it needs as much information as possible.

The theme: Why we chose what we chose.

The results: Don and Geraldine were able to sell their plans with but a few minor alterations.

The Presentation Analysis Form

To facilitate the process of developing a strategy, you may wish to tear out, enlarge, and work from the presentation analysis form on pages 220 and 221 in the appendix. Rather than write on the form itself, I urge you to use Post-it notes so that you can easily change your mind without confusing yourself with scribbles and pencil marks. Try to keep your thoughts in bullet points. Fill in all the boxes on the first page and then transfer them, where relevant, to the second.

PAGE ONE

Step one: Start with a description of who is in your audience.

Step two: Try to decipher your audience's carrots. I separate the professional from the personal even though both belong under the professional umbrella. *Professional* refers to the business itself; *personal,* to the individuals' goals and needs.

Step three: State your "to do." Remember: a "to do" is an action you want your audience to take after you have finished speaking. It does not refer to receiving applause or praise.

Steps four and five: Define your strategy. You may need to separate the conceptual part of your strategy from the proof.

Step six: Develop a theme, if possible.

Step seven: Set a tone or tones for the talk.

Step eight: Jot down the content or title of your talk.

Page Two

Before you begin working with this page, jot down on individual Post-it notes the points and subpoints that you intend to cover. Place the notes on the table or desk in front of you in any random order. This should become a sort of free-for-all, with random thoughts in random order. If you have a long presentation, work on one section at a time.

Now, take your theme or "to do" and, along with your audience's carrots, place them above the array of Post-it notes. Start moving those around until you develop a sequence that works with your audience's carrots and your "to do." This is another method of the cut-and-paste approach to creating a document.

Important: Anything that does not relate to your audience's carrots should be tossed out. That which is not relevant to your audience weakens the audience's desire to buy into your "to do."

The idea is to develop your content in line with your strategy, being mindful that strategy always takes into consideration your audience's carrots and your own "to do."

THE "SAY IT WITH CONFIDENCE"
PRESENTATION ANALYSIS FORM page 1

1

Who?

How many?

2A

What are your audience's **professional** "carrots" ?

2B

What are your audience's **personal** "carrots" ?

3
WHAT YOU WISH YOUR AUDIENCE *TO DO*.

What you want your audience to do AFTER you've finished speaking

3
YOUR STRATEGY (CONCEPT)

Use audience's "carrots" to entice toward your "to do."

3
YOUR STRATEGY (PROOF)

Visuals
Case histories

6
THEME

A theme runs through a presentation.

7
TONE

For instance: upbeat, serious, urgent, warning, excited

8
YOUR TOPIC

OVERALL VIEW of CONTENT

THE "SAY IT WITH CONFIDENCE"
PRESENTATION ANALYSIS FORM page 2

THEME	PERSONAL REMINDERS	OPENING
	SMILE **ENERGY** POSTURE	There are no rules. Possible openings: your "to do," your theme

POINT	1st SUPPORT POINT	2nd SUPPORT & TRANSITION

POINT	1st SUPPORT POINT	2nd SUPPORT & TRANSITION

POINT	1st SUPPORT POINT	2nd SUPPORT & TRANSITION

CONCLUSION

YOUR "TO DO" or
REITERATION
OF THEME.

One last thought to you and any creative directors who might be reading along: To sell is honorable; to be sold, divine—especially when the sell is artfully done. This means that you, the presenter, must pay close attention to your buyer's or audience's needs. It means that you fully accept the fact that any product, idea, or person, no matter how extraordinary, needs a spokesperson, and that this holds true even if the product is you. It also means that you should never forget that most audiences want to be sold—if not, they wouldn't be there.

CHAPTER 7

Misconception: "It's the content that counts."

I believe in content—substantive content. Without content a speaker lacks credibility. Without content an audience drifts off into self-contemplation. Content counts to such a degree that I have refused to take on clients because their content was antithetical to my beliefs. I feared that if I improved the speaker's style, audiences would buy what he or she espoused. I have seen speakers mesmerize audiences without content, with deceitful content, or with just plain outlandish content, and I have no desire to help proliferate sham. Oh, content counts, all right, but in this not the best of all possible worlds, style all too often holds sway over substance.

Did you know that audiences remember approximately 7 percent of what you say, 38 percent of how you say it, and 55 percent of what your body is doing? True! This means that if your body does something

147

just a little out of the ordinary, your audience may not even retain that lowly 7 percent. Remember how I managed to distract an audience by simply rubbing my finger around my thumbnail (chapter 4). However, because we learn more by doing than by listening, repetition, strong visual aids, and audience participation will increase the odds in your favor. Still, imagine how much content gets obliterated by poor speech, nervous mannerisms, or bad voice quality!

I often ask clients what they want from a speaker before a speaker speaks. The list we compile usually includes: a smile, eye contact, a confident (not cocky) manner, a cohesive appearance, someone who projects a strong desire to speak and . . . energy! The word *energy* should not be confused with *enthusiasm*. Energy fuels the entire range of emotions a speaker may need to project such as exhilaration, sadness, anger, and enthusiasm. Energy is what adds the spice to a speaker, no matter what the speaker's subject matter. (It also adds the spice to how we come across when we are silent.) Those who have energy—and can control it—attract; those who do not, may not repel, but can be easily overlooked. Harnessed energy is what creates charisma.

After a brief discussion we then extend the list to include what an audience wants once the speaker's mouth opens. The answers: someone who knows the material and can present it clearly and concisely, a strong interesting voice with clear enunciation, a wide range of vocal expression, interesting body language that doesn't interfere with content, and, of course, substance. Both lists describe a relaxed, confident, energetic, personality. (There's no conflict between

remaining relaxed and staying energized simultaneously. One can be—and should be—both at the same
time.)

We've already stated that confidence comes from
knowing what to do, learning how to do it, and then
doing it often enough so that you can do it with confidence. That's the inner piece of the pie, the piece
that should be recognizable on contact. However, as
was discussed in chapter 4, the interior self does not
always replicate itself externally. Highly confident
people can come across as uncertain and appre-
hensive, while the most insecure among us can
appear in control and confident. (See Maryann in
chapter 3, and Caroline in chapter 4.) To paraphrase
Molière, that which appears simple is most likely
not! My father used to say that you meet people by
their dress and leave them by their character. While I
believe there's more to it than that, the truth is that
first impressions can only be based on appearance and
manner, which is a combination of personal grooming,
wardrobe, body language, and mood.

We discussed eye contact in chapter 3, camou-
flaging and overcoming manifestations of nervousness
in chapter 4, and how to develop correct energy levels
and emotions and reflect them facially in chapter 5.
Some of the others we'll discuss here.

Appearance

Bill Gates can wear whatever he desires, and his audiences will accept that which he has to say about com-

puters, success, business, success, money, and success.
However, unless you have a reputation that greatly
precedes you, the more cohesive the picture you
present to your audience, the easier you make it for
your audience to buy into what you put forth. If you
visually confuse your audience, that is, if you don't
look the way your audience imagines a professional in
your field should look, your audience will concentrate
on "what's wrong with this picture" rather than listening to what you are saying. Each field has its own
wardrobe, and while parameters have loosened, there
are still rules of conformity. Those who dress "out of
field" send double messages. Sneakers may look good
on art directors, they do not add credence to a financial
consultant's advice. One school of thought espouses
that you should "mirror" your audience; I do not. I
believe that you should dress according to who you
are, but appropriate to the situation, much as you
would dress in private life—a swimsuit at the beach,
golf clothes on the golf course, business attire to
business. I did, however, see this last dictum carried to
a rather hilarious extreme a number of years ago, when
I attended a black-tie fund-raising event for the arts.
The hall was filled with New York's political and
business community, along with a large number of art
world superstars and aspirants. There was no need to
worry about who was who, especially among the men
in the crowd. The business folk wore traditional attire
(men: tuxedos; women: an array of gowns). The artists,
on the other hand, wore: tuxedo jackets over dungarees, Eastern styled lounging jackets again over
dungarees, saris over dungarees, and an incredible

array of obviously "artistic" conconctions. The pièce de résistance as far as I was concerned was that of one male artist, who I knew came from a monied background. Obviously torn between his parents' world and his own, he wore a full tuxedo, but put a tiny tear surrounded by smudges of paint in one sleeve.

Under appearance obviously comes grooming. I strongly suggest deodorant and any kind of underarm pads you may need if attacks of nervousness produce perspiration. Limit perfume or aftershave to the barest minimum, if used at all. Keep the hair under reasonable control. Women, touch up your makeup during the day; men, shave when necessary. Women, keep jewelry to a minimum, and no dangling bracelets—they distract. By the same token; men, empty thy pockets of jangling coins. For both sexes; there's nothing wrong in going to an image consultant with a proven reputation for tasteful choices.

Body Language

I take great exception to those who teach that we can read a person's character by reading his or her body language. We cannot! Crossed arms do not mean that someone is self-protective or angry; they simply mean that the person *appears* to be self-protective or angry. (Remember the anesthesiologist in chapter 5.) This said, it is still human nature to leap to conclusions about others, based on what they appear to be.

Don. Don's boss, who had inherited Don from his predecessor, found him to be "nervous, reticent."

When I inquired about Don's potential, his boss responded with "Who the hell knows? He's too damn retiring. And nervous! Boy, is he ever nervous." Enter Don. His physique was that of a high school or college football player; his voice, incongruously soft. His humor, however, was apparent immediately, and he injected it appropriately throughout the day. As the workshop progressed, we discovered that Don's voice grew even softer when he felt insecure with his material and softer still when speaking in front of "superiors," not because he felt inferior, but because he was raised—extraordinary in this day and age—to hold one's tongue when elders were present. In other words, his silences were cultural and not due to any inferiority complex or inadequacy. When I explained this to his boss, his reaction was "But what about his nervousness. I mean, his hands shake!" They did, but this too was not from nervousness. They shook due to four concussions suffered on the football field. Surprisingly, Don's hands appeared calm when they were placed against an object such as his lap or a table. I explained this also to Don's boss, but he still preferred to take a wait-and-see attitude; he'd wait and see if Don would strengthen his voice, become more animated facially, and use his hands less before he'd make a final assessment of Don's abilities and potential.

We could label shaking hands as overt body language, but we judge others on much more subtle clues than that: the way they tilt their head, hold their shoulders, use their hands, position their feet, or purse their lips. If you have any doubt, sit or stand in front of a full-length mirror. Keep your head absolutely straight. Now tilt it two inches to one side. Notice how your demeanor changes. Go back to the straight position and raise your chin approximately an inch. No matter what your height, you will appear to be looking down upon others. Now, compress your lips. A wee bit judgmental, no?

Posture

There's no way a speaker can project a confident self with poor posture. Rounded, sagging shoulders, a drooping stomach, and shuffling gait do not show a person who can take care of him- or herself, much less an audience. During the presidential campaign of 1988, I only half-jokingly maintained that Dukakis would lose his bid for the presidency because he kept his arms pressed close to his body, a posture that made him look like a victim. We do not trust victims to handle difficult situations. Certainly we do not expect victims to take care of us—they can't even take care of themselves. Audiences are no different from electorates. Both need to feel taken care of in order to be able to sit back, relax, and receive the message.

While I'm described by audiences as someone who gives off an aura of confidence—that is, I fit the description of a speaker who combines a strong physical presence with openness and high energy—the maintenance of good posture for me is a never-ending battle. Loose-limbed people such as myself usually find that their bodies tend to collapse upon themselves much like the Scarecrow's in *The Wizard of Oz*. Until an orthopedist explained that my long ligaments and weak musculature lay at the root of my problem, I had blamed my poor posture upon a too-early sprout, having towered over classmates from the age of eight. I had always assumed that my stooping—if not to conquer then at least to appear like a peer—along with my teenage proclivity to copy the model's slouch then in vogue, had contributed to my difficulty with maintaining decent posture. It wasn't as if parents, teachers, and even friends hadn't tried to improve the way I held myself. I had my back prodded by the best of them until, in a grand attempt to change, I took to walking around the house with a book balanced on my head.

Consider this: The neck, the uppermost part of the spinal column, carries on its end our head, which contains 10 to 15 percent of the body's total weight. If the neck is out of alignment, the head will tilt, forcing the rest of the body to compensate for the imbalance. This is why I ended up compensating for my oval dome by tilting my jaw too high, arching my back, and doing whatever other contortions were necessary to keep the bloody book in place. This self-imposed attempt at correct alignment wasn't as horrendous as what Eleanor Roosevelt had to endure. According to Blanche Wiesen Cook's biography, she was made to "walk up and down the River Road for hours at a time, with a stick behind her shoulders, hooked at her elbows." I've tried it. It produces a Dolly Parton–like bustline—in male and female alike—as well as a sore neck and aching shoulders.

Good Posture Has Nothing to Do with Books and Sticks, but with Movement

With the writing of this chapter, my posture has once again improved, surprisingly, with very little effort. Once you know what should be done, a simple reminder can be all that's necessary to put it into effect. Keep in mind that good posture allows the lungs room to breathe and the spine to elongate rather than compress, and, if it is correctly achieved, it can alleviate tension.

We usually approach posture with the concept that it is stagnant. We hear those voices from our past telling us to "sit up straight! Put those shoulders back! Keep the buttocks in!" and we then hit the pose and tighten up. However, that is not only exhausting, but also, for many of us, impossible to maintain. The trick to good posture is to think of it as a continual outward movement of all body parts; a fluid movement outward; a relaxation—not a collapse—of the muscles of the body. See if you can decompress your head from the neck, allowing it to float up toward the ceiling. Do the same with your shoulders to the opposite walls. Keep your stomach relaxed. Do NOT suck it in! Holding in the stomach inhibits proper breathing. Allow your rib cage to expand. (In order to know how an expanded rib cage should feel, put your hands high up around the sides of your ribs and breathe in.) Then stretch your spine so that the vertebrae cannot touch; however, make certain you do not arch the back. Do not forget to include the legs; they too get stretched. If you truly want to develop good posture, I suggest that you find an instructor certified in the Alexander Technique, developed a hundred or so years ago by F. Matthias Alexander, an Austrian actor. I have seen clients for whom maintaining a decent alignment meant agony emerge with a comfortable and easy stance. There are a number of books on the subject, but even these stress that it is safer and more beneficial to work with an expert than to go it alone. The Alexander Institute in New York City will be glad to refer you to licensed practitioners in your area.

Now, although we tend to think of posture as residing mainly in the spine and shoulders, it encompasses the entire body including its appendages. So, feet first:

Feet

Stand in front of the mirror or, if you wish, just stand in place and look down. Point your toes inward; now outward. Notice the different image you project. Too far in, you appear introverted; too far out, a bit like a ballet dancer or a duck; straight ahead and just slightly turned out, you appear, for lack of a better word, normal. It's subtle, but it can make a difference in how you come across to others, whether you are standing or sitting. When they sit, many people bob their feet either as a way to keep their circulation going or simply out of a nervous habit. The habit distracts! Even if the bobbing is done under a table, others notice it. The upper body moves, and/or the chair squeaks. Better to learn how to tighten and relax the muscles in the leg rather than jiggle them.

Hands

While audiences should focus on a speaker's words and facial expressions, our fingers and hands can easily upstage both. Hands that are too active or, for that matter, lifeless, distract. Hands that extend the speaker's words, that are in tune with the speaker's feelings, enhance. Hands and fingers should serve as punctuation marks, and when they are appropriate and not corny, should work as visual aids to reinforce the text. They should not—unless we're speaking to the hearing impaired—be used for sign language. They should also be kept within the audience's peripheral vision of your face.

If you have a problem controlling your hands, that is, if the fingers of each hand seem drawn to each other like magnets, or clasp in a wringing motion, or remain fixated in front of your crotch (known in the trade as the fig leaf position) or hidden behind you (causing your audience to wonder whether you are about to spring a surprise or are doing something behind your back that should better be kept secret), or if your hands hang limply at your sides, or worse, hang from your wrists, get some weights. Practice speaking with one weight in each hand. You claspers may wish to start with two glass goblets and switch to weights once you've broken the clasping habit. By adding weight and remembering that your hands are meant to extend your feelings, you will begin to know what your hands should feel like even when empty, and you will begin to use them with controlled energy. Recently I have begun adding ice cubes to the glasses as a way of helping clients to learn how to control arm and body movements. The trick is to use the arms while making certain that the ice cubes remain silent.

Lips

Although they are not considered an appendage, what you do with your lips when you are not speaking can entice or put off others. In complete contrast to the admonition "Close your mouth or you'll catch flies," keeping your mouth slightly ajar—and the emphasis is on *slightly*—makes you appear more accessible. Closing your lips tightly over your teeth may be more comfortable—here again, a mirror helps—but it usually looks as if you are judgmental, withholding, or withdrawn.

Voice

Pity the poor audience who must listen to a speaker whose voice grates or is nasal, or who slurs or swallows words; who cannot raise volume without yelling or lower it and still be heard; who cannot control the pace—racing through the content with the speed of lightning so that not one thought is transmitted to the audience; or a speaker who inappropriately slows down with a range of tone so narrow that it rocks the audience to sleep. Pity the wasted content.

I am continually fascinated as to how much time people spend creating presentations, sometimes working and reworking the material up to the very last minute, and then blow it all with poor enunciation, lack of intonation, no vocal contrast, and poor pacing.

The number of things that cause us to speak as we do can be as vast as each individual's experience. For instance, a soft-spoken manner can be cultural. A Japanese friend of mine answers the phone much as a Westerner might expect a geisha to sound. With a delightfully soft singsong lilt, which starts low and ends high, she coos, "Helloo," and then the moment she hears it's me, she gives out a midrange matter-of-fact, rather flat "Oh, hi." It took me a while to realize that the change of tone and octave had to do with her American voice and not disappointment at finding me on the other end.

A soft voice can be environmentally caused; those raised in households with a sick family member usually tiptoe and shush each other until eventually anything uttered above a whisper sounds like a scream.

A soft voice can be physiological; although by and large I have found that those who sound as if they have no voice usually house quite the opposite. I had one client who spoke in the tiniest pipsqueak. However, when something comical occurred, catching her off guard, out came an enormously loud guffaw, which startled all around her. The first time I heard this, I realized just how large a voice she actually had, one that she would have to learn how to control. Once she learned how to control her breath, supporting her voice with an expanded rib cage and strong stomach muscle control, she was able to modulate her voice appropriately from soft to loud.

Of course, a soft voice can be psychological; someone who was continually corrected by parents or teachers may race through or mumble the material trying to avoid the expected criticism.

Krasne's law: If you open your mouth to say something, then say it so that others can understand it. Forcing others to strain to decipher the sounds you make is rude, much like offering a plate of hors d'oeuvres and then pulling it away before the guests have a chance to pick one up and eat it. Just as hungry guests will eventually leave to find food elsewhere, an audience will tune out and mentally go elsewhere for sustenance. An audience only stays with a speaker with clear enunciation, and falls behind one who drops syllables and sounds. If the audience falls behind once too often, it tunes out entirely.

An energized voice, wide range of intonation, variety of inflection, and stress patterns keep an audience awake.

To find out how you sound, record a telephone conversation with a good friend. Wait a week; then play it back. If your friend sounds like your friend, that other voice you hear is the voice others hear when you speak. If you like what you hear, great! If you don't, get to work.

The exercise I use personally to get into vocal shape, and one that I urge on my clients, is based on Demosthenes, the Greek orator, who, according to history, originally had a weak voice along with a speech impediment. Wanting to communicate his thoughts to others, he went down to the sea, put pebbles in his mouth, and forced himself to speak loud and clear over the roar of the waves. It worked! Rather than pebbles, which, if you swallowed them, could cause a few problems, I recommend using your fingers. Here's how it works.

EXERCISE.

1) Put all five fingers in your mouth.
2) Keep your teeth off your fingers—the exercise is difficult enough without bloody knuckles.
3) As long and as loud as you can, enunciate each sound of each syllable of whatever reading material you have around. For now, try the following sentence:
   THIS IS A REAL-LY DIFF-I-CULT EX-ER-CISE TO PER-FORM, BUT E-VEN-TU-AL-LY I WILL GET IT.
4) Immediately after, repeat the sentence without trying to manipulate your mouth.

Your voice will only improve if you exaggerate each sound in each syllable. For instance, -*cise* as in *exercise,* should be pronounced making certain that the *s* sound at the beginning of the syllable, the *i* in the middle, and the *z* sound at the end are overpronounced and extended to their fullest. The more you do this, the more you will hear an improvement in your voice. I suggest doing this at least five minutes each day. If this is done correctly, your voice will sound slightly stronger and your enunciation will be clearer.

Accents

For the most part, I like them. Regional speech and dialects are what distinguish us from each other. I am appalled when I turn on TV and cannot tell the difference between one announcer's voice and another. There are now at least ten Jane Pauleys, four Barbara Walterses, Lord knows how many Peter Jenningses, and so forth. What happened to old Chet, David, and Walter, whom we could recognize with our ears only? Having stated that, I do make distinctions between regionally educated and noneducated speech. In other words, like it or not, there are class distinctions in speech, and I prefer to aim upward rather than down. This does not mean we should aspire to pseudointellectual or high-falutin' lingo; simply the best sounds our particular regions have to offer are usually acceptable nationwide. Also, if you have to cross borders a great deal between north and south, east and west, you may need to make a few adjustments, such as slowing down or speeding up, dropping some colloquial expressions, and double-checking your audience to make certain that you're being understood.

Projection

When I started in the theater, we did not use microphones. Singers, actors, performers stood onstage and could be heard in the last row of the balcony. We sang—with a full orchestra in front of us—and projected our voices so that others could hear us, no matter where they sat. We did not yell; we visualized where the sound had to go and sent it there, the same way you would throw a ball to someone. We could throw hard or soft balls, raising our voices in anger or bringing them down to a whisper. No matter which, our "balls" reached their targets. They did so because of a combination of 1) clear enunciation—each sound of each syllable was decipherable; 2) an awareness on our part of needing to communicate with our audience; and 3) a controlled energy level that allowed the sound to carry.

Of course, all voice is supported by breathing. Here's one breathing exercise that can help you learn to control your breath.

EXERCISE: BREATHING.
(Wear nonconfining clothing for all breathing exercises.)

1) Lie on back on the floor, a couch, or a firm mattress.
2) Place one hand on your diaphragm and one on your chest.
3) Breathe in slowly through your nose. Expand your stomach as if it were a balloon.

Hand on chest should not move.

4) Exhale through your mouth. Your abdomen should sink in. Keep trying until it does. Do not move your chest. **Repeat until mastered.**

5) Repeat steps 1–4, counting silently as you go. Take in as much air as possible. When you have reached your limit, press in with your palms in order to push out the air that is left.

6) Repeat step 5. This time, push your stomach up toward the ceiling, as you let out a loud strong "AH." Keep your throat open.

7) Work toward: 4 *slow* counts on inhale; 8 *slow* counts on exhale.

8) When this is mastered, and only then, try doing it sitting up and, eventually, standing.

Concentrate on:

1) Making sure your diaphragm is moving in the right direction.

2) Regulating your counts.

3) Keeping your throat and jaw relaxed at all times.

One last very important point: Never, ever use your throat to change the pitch of your voice or to increase volume. The throat should always be kept open. Using your throat to make sound causes damage—possibly permanent—to your throat. If you suffer from hoarseness, nasality, or the like, you should seek a certified speech therapist who will most likely take you on only after a medical doctor has ascertained that there are no physical problems such as nodes on the vocal cords, or a deviated septum.

For those of you interested in going further on voice and enunciation on your own, I recommend Lyle V. Mayer's *Fundamentals of Voice & Diction*. I find his techniques by far the most effective.

CHAPTER 8

Misconception: "I must appear professional."

I've watched people of all ages behave, forgive me, as if they had a rod up their you-know-what, speak in a language that only their particular "in" group could understand, while putting on some of the most convoluted presentations anyone could possibly imagine— all in a sincerely earnest attempt to appear "professional." Not my word—theirs. So that we're clear:

A *professional* is someone who **has** expertise.

A *presenter* is someone who **shares** that expertise with others.

A *professional presenter* makes certain the audience **gets** the information.

A *pseudo-professional presenter* is someone who wants to **show off**.

Pseudo-Professional Presenter Speak

Imagine being on the receiving end of this verbatim quote, which a client of mine had planned to say: "When we last met, there was universal buy-in to our positioning recommendation, but before we moved forward, we agreed to do consumer research." To paraphrase the bard, while my client was anything but an idiot, his sentence signified nothing. "When we last met" sounds like a lyric from a schmaltzy song and speaks *at* rather than *with* an audience; "there was universal buy-in" employs the extremely aloof third-person voice rather than the more conversational first, and "but before we moved forward" misleads: 1) if the *d* of *moved* is not fully enunciated, it sounds as if the speaker is about to go off on a tangent (try saying it aloud); and 2) the *but* changes the sentence's meaning. What my client meant to say—and, thankfully, did— was: "The last time we were together, we all agreed to the positioning strategy and to conduct consumer research." It was clear and concise, and, therefore, his audience could get it.

I know that those who fall into the pseudo-professional trap wish to appear knowledgeable. Often, like many of us, they associate intelligence with high and mighty verbiage. Professor, writer, and recipient of a 1995 MacArthur Fellowship, Patricia Nelson Limerick describes this phenomenon in one of the most incredibly on-target (as well as humorous) pieces written on unintelligible writing. Limerick's hypothesis, as cited in an essay adapted for the *New York Times,* is that "dull difficult prose can function as

a kind of protective camouflage." She asserts that such
prose is taught at the college level by professors who
develop their own unintelligible language in an
attempt to overcome their feelings of shame at not
being more socially adept. Put another way, unintelligible language is one way of rejecting someone before
that person can reject you. Although she is concerned
with academia and academic prose, Limerick's ideas
easily translate to the world of business outside her
ivied walls. Over and over again I find inexperienced
as well as experienced speakers using language that
only a colleague who has stopped listening for com-
prehension could love. One freelance writer told me of
being in a meeting in which a director of marketing
stood up and declared, "We will tell our clients that
we're going to give the consumer permission to
believe." Everybody except the freelance writer
beamed with approval as if the sentence actually had
meaning.

There are times I'd prefer to wrest a security
blanket from a toddler rather than separate a client,
intent on appearing professional, from his or her own
particular form of pseudo-professionalism. Everyday
speech, I'm told, is fine for every day but not under
any circumstances, for presentations. One highly self-
contained financial marketer disintegrated before my
eyes as I reworked his portfolio manager's presentation
to make it more user friendly. With arms crossed,
teeth clenched, and in a voice that verged on mild hys-
teria, he declared, "She can't sound uneducated!"
Informed that this would not occur, he continued to
do battle with me over the format, the language, the

design of the slides and even the rehearsal process itself. Only after he was barred from the sessions and I had the freedom to work unimpeded with the portfolio manager—reworking her presentation's sentence structure until, finally, it matched her own speech patterns—could I prove to them both that using words and phrases that no one but a lexicologist can grasp does not make one sound intelligent, only unintelligible. Or, as another client put it, "In trying to appear professional I devised highly complex sentences. Hey, they sounded great to me. What a helluva surprise to find out no one understood a word I was saying."

The purpose of language is to communicate. Whether we have been brainwashed by academia into thinking that convoluted speech shows intelligence, or whether we use it to protect ourselves from being questioned on our content, or whether we simply have fallen into bad habits by using our own industry's shorthand indiscriminately, the truth is: **Unintelligible presentations do not transmit information, and information that is not transmitted cannot be bought or bought into.**

Think about it this way: If you know what you're talking about, you can be clear about what you know, which means that if you speak with clarity, others just might assume that you know something.

The Pseudo-Professional Presentation

The incomprehensible complex sentence is only topped by the incomprehensible, complex visual aid.

A *visual* is something that pertains to seeing; an *aid*, something that helps or supports. If a visual aid does not assist a speaker in getting the message across, if it does not help an audience to get a speaker's message, then it is a hindrance, and a hindrance cannot be an aid.

Many people are under the assumption that the more complex the visual aid, the more professional-looking the presentation and, in turn, the more professional the presenter. *Dumb!* Where visuals are concerned, complexity only obscures. As a matter of fact, the more complex any issue is, the clearer and more linear you need to be in its presentation.

Now, there was a time when few if any visual aids were used in presentations, and those that were either would be considered primitive by today's standards (the blackboard and flip chart) or too costly and time consuming (slides). Then two things happened: 1) Technology made the production and reproduction of visual aids easier, faster and cheaper, and 2) a series of studies, conducted mostly by universities, appeared that concluded, or were interpreted as concluding, that if they used visual aids, presenters would come across as more professional and therefore would be more effective. The word spread: If you want to appear professional, pile on the visual aids. And everybody did, whether they were called for or not. Today visual *non-aids* abound: overloaded slide trays, information-overloaded slides, slides filled with undecipherable graphs and charts, unoriginal computer-generated graphics—and the list goes on. Hardly anyone thinks about whether or not visuals are needed, only about how many should be used, a rather ironic situation in this era of downsizing and cost-effective fixations. I suggest that before you rush to include visuals in your next presentation, you take a look at what the studies did and did not conclude.

THE "LEARNING" STUDIES

An army study stated that people retain facts up to 55 percent longer when they are able to see as well as hear the presented material (Ronald E. Green). A doctoral thesis from Arizona State University asserted that typing skills are increased when typing is taught with a sound/slide package (Joyce Kupsh). A study from the University of Wisconsin determined that learning improved up to 200 percent when visual aids were used in teaching vocabulary, and Harvard and Columbia found that audiovisuals improved retention from 14 percent to 38 percent (Tom Colthran). Each in its own way, concluded that we learn better and retain information better when more than one of our senses is engaged. Granted. There's no argument that the more our senses become involved when we take in information, the more information we will retain. But, not every presentation is a teaching presentation. When we are presenting a product or an idea, we are asking our audience not to learn but to buy. As we've seen in previous chapters, in order to buy, an audience needs to have a rapport with the presenter. If the intent of the presentation is simply to shove information into an audience's brain, then hell, bombard the listeners from all fronts. But if the intent of a presentation is to sell, then the speaker needs to build a relationship, one that, hopefully, will continue past the presentation itself. That cannot, nor will not, occur if the visual aids take center stage over the presenter.

THE "BUSINESS" STUDIES

With the rise of MBA programs, academia brought its hypotheses to the business community. "A Study of the Effects of the Use of Overhead Transparencies on Business Meetings" by the Wharton School asserted that the use of an overhead projector could influence a meeting's outcome. A study conducted by the University of Minnesota with the 3M Company concluded that presenters who used visual aids had a better chance of selling their ideas than those who did not, and that an average presenter with visual aids was graded as equal to that of an above average presenter without visual aids. Interestingly, in the opening of the University of Minnesota/3M study, referring to the Wharton School study, there's a sentence that could be applied to all the studies, the UM/3M study included. It is: "Frequently the claims exceed the study's explanatory capabilities." In the Wharton case, I believe it's the interpretations of the study that exceed the study's capabilities, not the study itself. For instance, the Wharton Study was designed to look only at the effect of visual aids on an audience, yet David Peoples, an author/trainer of presentation skills, uses the study to prove his theory that it's better to stand than to sit when presenting. Although in the study the presenters with visual aids who happened to stand got higher acceptance ratings than those presenters without visual aids who presented sitting, the study itself never drew such a conclusion. It couldn't. That would require another whole study. (The study does suggest that others conduct research regarding the relationship between group size and the effect of overheads, what happens when all presenters use overheads, as well as the impact of overheads with other technologies.)

My main problem with the Wharton study is the fact that all the participants were MBA students who, although they may have had prior exposure to marketing cases and/or some business experience, were playing the part of marketing managers. In other words, they were still in the learning phase of their careers. They were used to sitting in classrooms and taking in information; used to having to listen, retain, and then process back. These MBA students were not on overload, as so many business executives are. Nor were they jaded by overexposure to presentation after presentation, meeting after meeting, salesperson after salesperson, which is not to say that their reactions were invalid, just that the data compiled might have been quite different if the study had used overworked, overtired business types instead.

If I have problems with the Wharton study, I'm astounded by the University of Minnesota/3M study, the one most often quoted, the one from which come the figures that support the conclusion that presentations with visual aids are 43 percent more persuasive than those without. I'm astounded because, in what well may have been a valiant attempt to make certain that individual performance could not be a variable, the authors of the study chose to videotape all the presenters whether they were using black-and-white transparencies, color slides, charts, graphs, or all or none of the above. In other words, while the study was looking at what role visual supports play in persuasion, it inadvertently turned the presenter (persuader) into another visual. Because any interaction between speaker and audience was eliminated, as far as I'm concerned, the conclusions were thoroughly skewed. Again, audience involvement changes audience response. There's a reason evangelic preachers ask audiences to stand up and shout "Hallelujah!" rather than simply sit and listen. The audience in the UM/3M study was passive, it was not called upon to interact, only to sit silently in judgment. Therefore, the power of the visuals could not be accurately accessed. Another gem is their second conclusion: "The persuasive impact of a presentation depends on characteristics of the support used. Presentation support in color is more persuasive than that in black and white. Image enhanced graphics are effective only when used selectively and carefully. Use of overhead transparencies results in the presenter being perceived as more interesting but less professional compared to the use of 35 mm slides." Books upon books have been written on color theory. Artists have struggled with the properties and impact of color for centuries. We all have different responses and preferences where colors are concerned. To state that color wins out over black and white is an incredible overstatement. When used properly, black and white can be highly effective if for no other reason than to single one presentation out from the crowd. (Yes, I am one of those who believe that the colorization of classic films has destroyed the brilliant images that the original filmmakers intended.) If your competitors all use blue screens with yellow letters, your client might well remember the one presentation that used a black screen with white letters underlined in red. Not that all colors are equal; certain colors can have a negative impact, while others can battle each other to such a point that they wipe each other out. It is interesting to note that while we read black print on a white page easily, and black print on an overhead projector, the intensity of a slide projector's light dilutes the black and enhances the white to such an extent that white type on a black screen is far preferable. As for color slides, if it takes a darkened room to decipher the slides, then the speaker will be unable to read or engage the audience clearly, making the slides, rather than the speaker, the focal point.

Most studies come about because someone wishes to prove or disprove a hypothesis. It must have been very difficult for those from the 3M Corporation, a company with an enormous investment in visual aid equipment and materials, to remain totally neutral in setting up the study. We can also presume that due to the resources at their disposal (that is, 3M's equipment and technical staff), they were able to produce visuals that consciously or unconsciously would prove their point. Therefore, the statement that a typical presenter has nothing to lose by using presentation support presumes that the presenter has access to high-quality visuals, is adept at using visual aids, will not fumble the overheads or become so nervous as to become totally out of sync with the slides, and can maintain eye contact with the audience and only glance at, not speak to, the screen itself. Even if the visuals themselves are well designed and produced, there still is a technique to working with them, one that must be learned and practiced. Still, my favorite conclusion is the one that states that better presenters need higher-quality visual support. Whether intentional or not, it certainly sounds more like a marketing ploy than proof of a hypothesis.

Even assuming that the study was unbiased, what concerns us here is not the study and its conclusions, but how those conclusions and the various (mis)interpretations have filtered into the business community. For instance, more time and effort now go into creating slides, overheads, and multimedia graphics for speakers than is spent by speakers in developing presentations and preparing to communicate to an audience. Scarier, one multimedia production house told me that 60 to 80 percent of its business comes from revisions, most of them made at the last minute. Because technology has made the creation of visuals affordable and fast, presenters can rework the visual aspects of their presentations right up to the last minute, which, as we'll see in the next chapter, can lead to disastrous results. As if that were not enough, because these changes do not allow rehearsal time, many presenters have now adopted a horrendous practice. They are writing out their entire script onto the slides themselves. Their excuse? It's the only way they can remember what they need to say. They forget that:

Audiences cannot read and listen at the same time.

We all read at different speeds. Some of us need to reread. Some of us speed-read. Listening to someone read something while we are read to can cause us incredible irritation. If you have any doubts, ask someone to hold up a book or magazine article and orally present the content to you while you try to follow along. I don't care whether the person speaks the exact words or talks about what is written on the slide. Either way, I have never known anyone not to find the speaker's voice an intrusion. If a speaker speaks too fast, you feel like an idiot for not grasping the information quicker. If the speaker speaks too slowly, the tendency is to attempt to block the speaker's voice from penetrating your psyche. In other words, just like a double negative, the speaker and the slide cancel each other out.

I am not against visual aids. They can add to most presentations, provided they are used judiciously, and yes, they can enhance certain presentations and even certain presenters, provided the visuals are appropriate to the subject, appropriate to the audience and to the occasion. You do not look professional using visuals indiscriminately. All a presentation crammed full of visuals tells your audience is that you've spent money indiscriminately and that you've learned how to use a slide projector or computer software program. On the other hand, you will look professional if your visuals help make your message clear. Words may stimulate an image; the word *tree* will evoke the image of a tree, but the image itself, a picture of a tree, requires far less time for the brain to process. Also, you will look professional if you do not allow your visuals to overshadow you. No visual can or should make up for what you lack. Keep in mind that you will always be your own best visual aid. This being so, it is the one you should spend the most time refining.

Pseudo-Professional Demeanor

According to my *Random House Dictionary*, a *professional* is a person who follows "an occupation as a means of livelihood or for gain"; someone who "belongs to a profession." It does not mean a style of dress, a manner of speaking, a way of writing, an attitude. Yet, as we've just seen, in attempt to appear professional, the pseudo-professional presenter bombards the audience with convoluted sentences, supports those sentences with indecipherable, complex slides, and, as if that's not enough, tops it off with a distant, rod-up-the-you-know-what demeanor and then wonders why the audience's eyes have glazed over. A remote demeanor does not win friends or influence anyone. It turns most people off. We saw, in chapter 5, that 1) our facial expressions and body language can either entice or turn off an audience to us, our ideas, or our product; 2) our moods color how we receive information; and 3) moods are contagious. This means that we, as presenters, have the power to put our audience in the mood we desire by getting into that mood ourselves. Because we do not wish our audience to be aloof to our ideas, an aloof pseudo-professional persona can only work against our ideas' finding acceptance. One client, a magazine editor, attested to this fact after attending a workshop. She wrote: "How devastating to find that others interpreted my demeanor as unfriendly and static. I'd worked so hard to make it 'professional.'" This particular client happened to be female. I say "happened to be" because the adoption of a remote demeanor in an attempt to appear professional, while prevalent in women who must compete in what was once termed a man's world, is by no means confined to them. I watched a wonderfully warm, friendly, outgoing man turn into an automaton the moment he got up to present, because, as he later told me, that's how he had been taught to present in college. My workshop was the first refresher course he had taken in twenty years, and he was shocked to learn how much his style of presentation had worked against him.

As has been shown elsewhere in this book, the reasons behind someone's behavior can be as simple as a bad lesson learned or as complex as the ones brought to me by another client who had spent years uncomfortably acquiring a professional mask. She had worked her way up the ladder at a social service agency, from secretary to fund-raiser. Her stated reason for attending my workshop was that she wished to overcome her fear of presenting to the agency's high-powered, wealthy, "difficult" board of directors. Her desire to come across in a manner that she perceived to be proper resulted in a strange, awkward presentation of self, reminding me of someone who must constantly maneuver a slippery sidewalk, her persona extremely careful, almost wary. This was exemplified by, but not confined to, her speech: a Brooklyn accent made all the more apparent by her attempt to camouflage it. One changes an accent by pinpointing the identifying sounds and then changing them to the desired ones. Too often, people try to correct an accent by overlaying it with what they perceive to be the proper sounds and end up with affected-sounding speech. Her high anxiety level during the first session made it difficult to break through her insistence that if she "just learned to control my nervousness," all would be well. I decided to lay the groundwork in the first session and tackle the core problem in subsequent ones, when some of her anxiety had abated and more trust had been established. In the next session I had her describe in detail each board member—the way he or she dressed, talked, interacted. It became quickly apparent that she was focused totally on their status, their money, schooling, upper-class mores. I threw caution to the wind and pointed out that no matter how she tried, she would never be a part of the board's social world. She said yes, she knew that. I then asked why she was continuing to try. She said she just wanted to be accepted. I explained that by seeking the board's acceptance on what she believed to be their terms, she only added to the extreme discomfort she was experiencing. Very few people enjoy being around someone who is constantly seeking others' approval, which is why approval seekers usually receive the very rejection they try desperately to avoid. Excessive self-involvement repels; interest in others attracts. To put it another way, if you look for validation as you speak, then you are not focused on delivering the message to your audience. By pretending to be something she was not, my client was actually inviting their ridicule, which only added to her insecurity. I urged her to allow herself to be herself. She had earned her stripes and should bask in that fact. She didn't need the Gucci bags and shoes to be accepted in her job—only expertise on how to raise additional funds for the agency. So what if she was from the so-called wrong side of the tracks? She was bright, had worked her way up on her own, was not handed anything on a silver platter. What was she hiding? There was one moment I will never forget, when the light went on and she seemed to shed layer upon layer of skin, or as she later put it, "I spent years hiding a major part of me—that street-smart gal from Brooklyn. The Eureka! came when you made it clear that professionalism means knowing your stuff, not pretending to be someone you're not." Which is not to say that she couldn't, if she wished, work on her accent with a speech coach or enhance her presentation style. Of course, she could, but what she had to learn was to build on who and what she was, not try to mask who she was behind a pseudo-persona. Before I sat down to write this chapter, I checked in with her. She expressed surprise at my timing, as earlier in the week one of the board members had made a point of telling her how much they all valued her input and professional expertise.

We all need to build upon who we are and not change into something we're not. When we remain true to ourselves, we present a cohesive message to our audience. When we pretend to be something we're not, we come across stilted in our presentation of self and materials. We consider those who speak in a down-to-earth style one moment and a mannered, poetic, or flowery style the next to be affected, and while we still may think someone affected, we do not think of them as phony when they maintain a consistency of style. Whatever your personal reactions to the following personalities, they are consistent: Jesse Jackson "preaches" whether he is sermonizing from a pulpit or fielding questions on a talk show; former New York Governor Mario Cuomo waxes eloquent on and off the platform, and William Buckley doesn't change his rather pedantic style, or so I'm told, even after two martinis. It is the smart professional who recognizes who he or she is and remains true to that self.

A few months ago I received a rather frantic call from a public relations person begging that I "do something." His CEO, whom I knew, had been asked to give a speech on cyberspace. The speech had been written by a well-known, well-paid speechwriter, and the CEO was having problems with it. Would I please do something to improve the CEO's presentation style? I asked to see the speech. Upon reading, I found it to be well researched, thought-provoking, and enjoyable to read, but it certainly didn't sound like the CEO I knew. He would never say words such as: "Before too long, we stand to face the challenge of engaging and communicating with a consumer universe, that is, by contrast, a mosaic made up of thousands of tiny pieces. A universe that is fluid in time, and changes composition constantly. That shows up one moment and disappears the next." I quickly realized that the CEO was having a difficult time because the speechwriter had asked him to speak in another language. Actors can learn to speak another's words and make it their own—although they should stop doing so once the curtain descends—but the rest of us find it hard to communicate in an alien tongue. The CEO was educated, and well versed in American speech; but to get his message across he needed to use his own words, words such as: "Before long we will all have to engage, and communicate with, an extremely diverse audience. It's going to be quite a challenge." Now, maybe this wasn't as poetic or even as well written as the original, but I was convinced that the CEO could learn it and deliver it with ease. More importantly, his audience would have no trouble believing that these words were his own—something it would have found hard to do if the CEO had delivered the first version and then responded in his own style during the question-and-answer period that followed. There was nothing wrong with the CEO's presentation style, only with the speechwriter's attempt to "elevate" the CEO's persona. The CEO already was a pro; he didn't need to sound like a pretentious one. He and I went through the speech line by line, converting each sentence and thought into his own phrasing. He had no trouble delivering the speech.

Creating the Professional Presentation

I am beginning to believe that half the problems associated with presentations would be done away with if more people would stop writing out their talks to be heard and instead chat their ideas into a tape recorder as if they were speaking to a friend over a sandwich and coffee. There's a difference between writing to be heard and writing to be read. Writing to be read allows for flowery or more formal prose, erudite words, uncolloquial expressions, and long, complex sentences (God help us all). We grant writers of the written word these liberties because we, the reader, can run to a dictionary, reread a sentence, or look up the chapter heading to search for the point the author might be attempting to make. A listening audience is denied such luxuries. Visual aids can work as content guides or supports for the material, but, as we've seen, they often work against rather than for the speaker. Also, we accept the fact that some people write in a different style than the one in which they speak. For instance, the speechwriter's version could have been published in a magazine, and no one, not even those who personally knew the executive, would have doubted the CEO's authorship. Interestingly, transcribing verbatim the spoken word to the written one does not work as well. During the writing of this book, a friend suggested that I'd speed up the task if I tape-recorded my seminars and then transcribed them. I roared. Besides the fact that workshops do not afford one the time to delve into subjects that a book does, when I am in front of a live audience, my facial and body language usually do most of my talking. My sentences can be quite casual. A lot of my content relies on reactions to immediate needs. What was taking me so much time was restructuring my thoughts for the written page.

It is the smart political speechwriter who creates one speech for the to-be-read news media and another for the politician to speak, and, while we may hear magnificent eloquence in an inaugural address, speeches of this type are written as much for the history books as for the immediate audience. In front of an audience I'd probably shorten the last thought to: "Politicians need one speech for the wires, and another for an audience," gesturing toward my audience to explain that I was referring to a live audience.

It's important to understand that if an audience is to accept your content, they must be able to accept you, which means that you must be consistent in your presentation of self and material. Audiences will spot pretension if you get up to speak in one tongue, such as pseudo-professional-ese, during your presentation, and another tongue, yours, during the Q&A. A good rule to follow is: If you are having a great deal of trouble learning the content, check the writing. If it doesn't sound like you, trash it!

Some additional notes on putting together a talk:

1) Speak your thoughts aloud into a tape recorder and then transcribe the tape, verbatim, onto the written page.
2) Organize and edit these pages, keeping the original sentence structure wherever possible. Print in caps,

double-space, and end each line where you would normally pause. This makes presentations easier to learn and helps break the habit of writing to be read rather than heard.

3) Use this version for the rehearsal sessions.

4) Pare these pages down to one- or two-word references in list form that could be, if needed, referred to during the actual performance.

Regarding visuals: use them judiciously. As my mother used to say, there's a time and place for everything. Visual aids that are clear, lively, and support the speaker add potency if for no other reason than that it appears that the speaker has put time and care into the preparation. So:

1) No sentences on slides; bullet points only.

2) Remember: a few bullets go a long way.

3) If you wish to interject humor, make sure it works!

4) Keep graphs and charts simple and easy to read.

5) Watch out for stock graphics; they can make you look run-of-the-mill.

6) Get creative, and when it's appropriate, break the rules.

One group of marketers, used to giving formal, detailed slide presentations to the sales force, were asked to "liven it up." While I couldn't get rid of the slides entirely, we edited them down, threw extraneous ones out, added banners and noisemakers (I'm serious), loosened up the presenters' style, and were a fantastic hit with the sales force who, I suspect, had expected to doze off. Granted, the marketers will be expected to top this the next time out, but creativity is not a one-time thing.

In other words, acquire the knowledge required to be a professional, share it in a clear, concise, down-to-earth manner, and you will be seen as the professional you will have become.

CHAPTER 9

Misconception: "Rehearsing makes me stale."

I have no studies to prove this, but I'm beginning to believe that most people loathe the rehearsal process as much as they fear speaking in public. The only tangible evidence I can offer to substantiate my belief is highly subjective and emanates from the fact that although I have trained thousands of people, I can clearly remember those few who truly comprehended what it means to rehearse correctly and did it willingly. Of course one could say that both go hand in hand, yet I find most people would rather "die" in public than take the steps that would assure them of, if not a winning performance, at least a passable one. I've been reduced to hounding clients with incessant phone calls after reason, cajoling, and emotional scenes have failed to move them to rehearse.

Certainly, one of the main reasons most people fear rehearsing is the same one that causes most people to avoid speaking in public in the first place: a fear of exposing one's inadequacies. However, whereas the fear of speaking in public emanates from the fear of exposing oneself to others, the dread of rehearsals has more to do with exposing oneself to oneself. This fear causes the person to put off as long as possible any concrete work on the presentation, finding excuse after excuse not to buckle down. It is not until the deadline looms and sheer panic sets in that work begins on the research, writing, and development of visual aids. Scant, if any, time gets paid to making certain that the presentation actually works or to securing the performance itself. Whatever time remains is usually given over to that wonderful stalling tactic of nitpicking. Then, if the presentation flops, well, lack of rehearsal time can be blamed and all illusions of self remain intact.

Before we go further:

To rehearse does NOT mean to memorize.

To rehearse does NOT mean to go over your speech in your mind.

And, NO, to rehearse does NOT mean to mumble the speech to yourself.

The rehearsal process is just that: a process. A process during which you:

1) Learn and internalize the material.
2) Develop and internalize complementary facial expressions and body language.
3) Create and internalize interesting vocal inflections.
4) Develop and internalize vocal patterns—deciding when and where to speed up, slow down, or pause.

Only when all the above elements are fully ingrained can everything be pulled together so that when you deliver the presentation, you can keep your focus on the audience and its needs rather than on your own. Omitting the rehearsal process leads to disaster.

The new business pitch debacle. The story I'm about to tell is true. As elsewhere in this book, certain identifying aspects have been changed to protect the guilty. However, although I've watched similar events take place in every industry, in this instance, I've chosen to keep one aspect of the story intact—that is, the fact that all the events took place at an advertising agency. I made this decision because: 1) Advertising people rehearse actors ad nauseam for every scene in every commercial they shoot. Ninety takes on even one line of copy mean nothing to those who write and produce commercials, yet they find even one run-through of their own presentations an intrusion on their time. In other words, they seem to understand the value of rehearsing for everybody but themselves; 2) most advertising new business pitches are more complicated than those required of other industries, and because they consist of many more elements, they allow us a more in-depth study of the presentation process; and 3) last-minute presentations are commonplace in the advertising industry, which means that working within tight time constraints is the norm.

On a Wednesday morning, the agency's director of new business, who knew that I had already held a number of presentation skills seminars at his agency, called to ask for my assistance on a pitch to be held the following Thursday. His agency had made it to the final round, and it was now down to his and three other agencies to compete for this particular piece of business. He wanted to know what I could accomplish given that we only had nine days and the pitch had yet to be written. I asked where they were in the process. That is, had the research been completed? The advertising and marketing strategies decided upon? Were the ideas for TV, radio, and print advertisements under way and the media plan drawn up? He said the research had been completed, a strategy was being worked out, the creative team was waiting on the strategy, and the media for the creative. He did, however, think that most of the segments would be written by the first of the week. Given that information, I suggested that I sit in on a run-through to make certain that the agency's thinking was coming across clearly and that the visuals were effective. I said I could also work with the presenters on their individual performances. We agreed to the following schedule:

1) Saturday–Sunday. Anyone whose section was near completion would run it by me over the weekend for content and editing of visuals.

2) Monday, 9 A.M. I, along with other people at the agency not involved with the pitch, would attend a run-through, during which we would ascertain whether or not the strategy to be recommended to the client was on target, and if the thinking behind it was clear. Then the presentation's strategy (not to be confused with the advertising strategy for the client's product) would be finalized and set in stone so all could go off and complete their sections. This would leave Monday afternoon/night, and Tuesday

morning, for revisions. I would be available to anyone who wished to work on his or her section.

3) Tuesday, 1 P.M. We'd hold a rehearsal that would also include reviewing the list of potential client questions. We would decide and rehearse in depth how they would be answered, and by whom.

4) Wednesday, 9 A.M. Technical run-through. All the visuals would be double-checked for accuracy, spelling, clarity, and order, and the audiovisual supports would be checked for quality and editing.

5) Wednesday afternoon. One last rehearsal. I would not attend, because at this stage presenters need to pull together and rely on each other rather than on a coach. I suggested they bring in available agency personnel to play "clients."

The schedule allowed for some technical fine-tuning Wednesday evening, a good night's sleep for the presenters, and some finishing touches, if necessary, Thursday morning before the clients arrived at 1 P.M. The pitch was to run a total of two hours, including time for questions and answers.

Now, I'm not naive. I knew the schedule would have to withstand some adjustments, but nothing could have prepared me for what actually did occur, especially since at the earlier seminars, attended by the top echelon from the president on down, everyone had appeared not only to endorse wholeheartedly the need to allocate time for rehearsals, but also to understand the dire consequences of omitting the rehearsal process. Heads had nodded in fervent agreement as I explained that:

1) If you don't know your material, you can't deliver it effectively, and if it isn't delivered effectively, no matter how wonderful it may be, it will fall flat.

2) If you do not feel confident—and there's no way you can be confident if you're winging it—it's impossible to think quickly enough to handle the incredible number of unexpected events that can, and usually do, occur.

3) Preparing for the question-and-answer period (which can take place during, rather than after, a presentation) is crucial to winning the business. This is where the presenters' competence is assessed. It is the make-or-break point of any new business presentation. If time has not been allotted for an in-depth rehearsal of potential questions and answers, all the work that has gone into the pitch itself can be lost.

4) Clients judge future performance on what they see, not what they're told. You can tell them you're a company of strong thinkers, that you're organized, creative, well managed, but if your presentation appears less than organized, if you can't stay within the time restraints set by the client, if the presentation itself does not appear creative, your words will fall on deaf ears. As an aside, this is true of any presentation, whether it's a job interview or a formal new business pitch. Audiences believe what you show them you can do, not what you say you can do.

As I said, heads had nodded, but in retrospect, I realized that was probably in recognition of past bad deeds rather than in agreement that their behavior should change. As the days rolled on, I witnessed the most ineffective modus operandi, made even more problematic by technology. Most companies whose business requires them to make numerous presentations now have in-house computer programs and technicians to run them. This means that changes can be made by simply typing them into the computer and clicking the mouse. Quite a change from the old days (as recent as fifteen years ago), when presentations requiring visual components were at the slide house months in advance and changes could push a budget over the top. Even ten years ago, changes on computers still required from twelve to twenty-four hours' turnaround time and plenty of extra dollars in the budget, which meant that at a certain point, a halt had to be called to making any alterations.

As you may suspect by now, the schedule to which the director and I had agreed existed solely to be broken. No one appeared over the weekend to rehearse or review his or her part. The Monday morning rehearsal took place Monday afternoon, and rather than being an actual rehearsal, it turned into a free-for-all discussion on alternative ideas. Even so, we managed somehow to set the strategy of the pitch, and everyone went off to work on their sections—or so I thought, until it became clear that the woman in charge of research and development had changed her mind. All on her own, without a word to anyone else, she decided that the marketing strategy should be altered. Her section became a private work of art to be worked and reworked until it achieved "perfection."

Worse, no one was in charge. The president was out of town; the director of new business was new on the scene; the man who was to handle the account and should have led the pitch turned out to be a close friend of the "strategist" and didn't feel "right" in taking over. It was anarchy. No one could or would stop the tinkering. The chaos continued into Wednesday, when the president returned. However, instead of saying "Enough!" he, too, got caught up with improving the "thinking" and tinkered even more. The first and only so-called rehearsal was held Wednesday night at 11 P.M. During this session the president's sections (the open and close) were written by committee. It got so late that some sections never even got a run-through. No thought was ever paid to the Q&A, and, at the only technical run-through, held at 9 A.M. the morning of the pitch, the creative director learned for the first time what the marketing director planned to say and went ballistic, believing it more appropriate for his section than for hers. Lack of sleep added to the stress. Everyone was on edge. The clients, all ten of them, arrived one hour early, just as the tech rehearsal finished.

Pleasantries exchanged, clients and presenters took their assigned places, and the pitch began. Adrenaline made up for exhaustion. The president officially opened and managed, incredibly, to stay within the allotted time frame. The second presenter didn't fare as well. Within a few minutes he realized that he was out of sync with his slides, became confused, and started to ramble, adding seven minutes to his section. The next presenter, in a desperate attempt to make up for the lost time, ran through her material at such a pace that no one could make head or tail of what she was saying. Then came the coup de grâce. The fourth presenter, in a grandiose attempt to save the day, got creative and threw into the mix a brand-new idea, one that never would have been allowed to see the light of day had it been discussed prior to the pitch. This idea hit such a raw nerve with the clients, who were sharply at odds about the particular issue, that an argument erupted among the clients themselves, ending with two of them storming out of the room. Needless to say, the agency didn't get the business. Of course, no one can say whether or not the agency would have won the business if they had rehearsed, but at least they wouldn't have ended up looking like incompetent scatterbrains.

Rehearsals are not exercises in vanity. They do not exist simply to enhance the way you perform. Their function is also to weed out problems, make certain that the content makes sense, that the presentation flows, and that it stays within the boundaries of time and content. Rehearsals give you the security of knowing that you do know what you're doing. They help you to appear confident, and, as we've said throughout the book, confidence sells.

No, rehearsals will not make you stale. We all have a story that we love to tell over and over. It might be just one or two sentences about our family, an incident that occurred in our youth, how we met a particular friend or lover, or it might be a joke which always gets a laugh. We tell it over and over and over again. It doesn't get stale. Usually, it gets better in the telling.

We add a little spice each time—a new inflection, a knowing look, a bit of embroidery.

Rehearsals differ from training sessions. Practice or training sessions are repetitions of specific techniques. Tennis players will practice their backhand, musicians scales, pitchers their fast ball. In the game of presentation skills, you practice your eye contact, facial expressions, body language, enunciation, voice quality—no specific presentation necessary. All you need is a mind set to work on these techniques in your daily life.

Rehearsals—now they're different. They need specific time periods during which you do nothing but focus on performing the presentation. Obviously, the longer and more complicated the presentation, the less experienced a presenter you are, the more time you'll need. However, a good rule of thumb is to set aside as much time as you will need to rehearse the presentation twenty times. That's right, TWENTY! I do not mean twenty times in a row, but certainly twenty over a period of days or weeks. As an example:

Gordie. An enormously talented industrial designer, Gordie had difficulty in showing passion. To say he undersold would be the understatement of the year. The more passionate he was about the subject, the less likely he was to be heard. Often he sounded as if he was taking his words back before they even got to his mouth. He wasn't bad one-on-one, if he felt comfortable with you and you leaned over to listen. Then, he could be quite articulate. He confided in me that he had a number of ideas that he desperately wanted to get across to others at the firm, ideas about how to make the firm more creative and profitable, ideas that I could tell he had thought about long and hard. I decided that Gordie needed a radical approach. I asked him to go home, jot down his ideas, organize them sequentially, and then list them as bulleted points. This would be his working script. Once it was completed, he was to begin saying his thoughts aloud. When he felt secure in his thinking, he was to repeat the process standing up, facing a wall with a pillow in his hand. On every point he made, he was to swat the wall with the pillow, hard! He was to do this over and over again until his voice and feelings hit the wall with the same intensity as the pillow. Only when his vocal and emotional energy started to click in was he then to practice giving the talk as if there were an audience present. Whenever he slipped in energy, he was to go back to using the pillow. He later told me that at take fifteen he thought he would never get it. It felt false, stilted. He was ready to give up. Then, on take twenty, something clicked. He couldn't explain what exactly the difference was, but all of a sudden, as he put it, "the words came out of me as if they were mine. I would never have believed it."

Gordie needed twenty takes to free his emotions so they could reinforce his words. He could have gone another twenty incorporating body language, eye contact, facial expression, movement. If he had stopped at take three or fifteen, before the clicking in occurred, he would have sounded stilted. We sound stale when we are low on energy, when we rehearse to ourselves, when we don't give it our all. It takes incredible energy to rehearse correctly. We sound stale when we don't add something to each rehearsal to enhance the telling, even if it is a new audience—imagined or real.

Karl (the man in chapter 6 who used as his theme to "grow a garden") during take seven added a hand movement for which he became known. At a particular point in the tour of the farm, he dramatically brought his hands together in a circle. It had nothing to do with gardening, but it was mesmerizing to watch. He told us later that he spent the first six takes in front of the mirror checking this and that until, suddenly, he hit upon this motion. He enhanced it through take ten, practiced his eye contact through take fifteen, added some new inflections, and finally watched it all come together about take twenty-two.

How to Rehearse

1) **Set a schedule.** Work backward from the date of the presentation. List the various aspects you will need to cover and divvy them up proportionately, leaving ample rehearsal time. If you plan to write your speech aloud, as suggested in the previous chapter, do not consider this part of the rehearsal period unless you stick with the script as originally conceived. Even if you only have a week, you may not skip a step, only shorten the time frame for each segment. The hardest part of creating a presentation is sticking to the schedule, but if you don't, you will not have time to rehearse, and all your work will be for naught. The most important date on the schedule is the one that

says: NO MORE CHANGES. I don't care what last-minute brilliant idea you think you have, if there's no time to internalize it, it will not sell.

2) **Rehearse OUT LOUD!** We do not think in complete sentences. Often we think without words at all. The French moralist Joseph Joubert supposedly said that we only know just what we meant to say after we have said it. Thinking and language do not necessarily go together. It takes practice to get our thoughts into phrases. My favorite client line: "Oh, I know just how I'm going to open my talk. Worked it out in my head on the way over." "Wonderful!" I say. "Let's hear it!" Out comes a series of false starts, *ums, ers,* and a "Well, I had it a minute ago." Turning abstract thoughts into succinct sentences requires trial, editing, and then repetition until you own the phrase.

There's another reason to speak the speech aloud and at a volume that assures your audience will be able to hear you. You need to be comfortable with the sound of your voice before you get up to speak. We don't pay attention to what our voice sounds like in the normal course of a day. We take our voice for granted the same way we do sitting, standing, or sipping a cup of coffee. It's what we do. If we add something special into the mix, though, such as speaking when others are silent, suddenly our voice can echo in our ears like the clanger of a bell at high noon, or sound as if it is coming from another planet. Either way, it brings with it the same wave of overwhelming embarrassment we felt when we were first called upon to answer a question at school. While in some cases familiarity may breed contempt, in this instance, familiarity breeds comfort. Our own voice heard on our answering machine, over time, becomes less alien. If we practice aloud our presentation at full volume, when we do speak while others remain silent, our voice will go back to being an accepted part of us, not something that causes additional self-consciousness.

I witnessed a man mumble his way through a talk that must have been written for him, or one that he silently pounded into his PC. When I was later introduced to him, he said, "Oh, you teach what I do so badly." I none too tactfully replied, "You would have done better to tear up the pages and talk directly to your audience." "Oh, but then I would have forgotten what I planned to say," he said. I held my tongue, but I desperately wanted to explain that a lapse of memory on his part would have been less painful to watch.

3) **Visualize!** This is not doublespeak. You visualize along with, not instead of, rehearsing aloud. If you know the room you are to present in, visualize yourself in it. Visualize the audience. Visualize where you will be sitting, where you will be standing. B. R. Bugelski (*The Psychology of Learning Applied to Teaching*) has shown how visualization can improve performance. Visualization can help you get over the heebie-jeebies by exorcizing them during the rehearsal process so that they will not exist, or at least will be minimalized in actual performance. Still, when it comes to public speaking, the doing

itself will save you, so, if you can get into the actual room and rehearse before the presentation, that will help enormously. Hotels and convention centers are quite amenable to allowing people into the rooms between events for a quick rehearsal.

4) **Work with a mirror.** Do this only for part of the time. The mirror is there to help you see yourself the way others will see you. It's a place to experiment with posture, hand movements, even facial expression. Do not get glued to the mirror, because if you do, then when you stand in front of the audience your best friend will no longer be there for moral support. Use the mirror the way dancers do. Dancers, whether in class or rehearsal, standing or moving, constantly check the mirror to scrutinize their form. If they are trying to attain an imperceptible curve from shoulder to fingertips, they will look to see if the shoulder is down, the arm extended, the elbow to the back wall, the top of the wrist on a diagonal to the ceiling, the palm on a lesser diagonal to the floor, the fingers extended with the thumb reaching toward the middle finger. Once the position is achieved, they memorize the sensation. It becomes so encoded in their body that even without a mirror, the exact position can be hit at any moment—in a moment. In other words, dancers use the mirror so that eventually they won't need it. I'm aware that it can be difficult to overcome the feeling of self-consciousness that working to a mirror can cause; however, if you look at it with an objective eye, then the mirror can be an incredibly helpful tool.

You may have noticed that nowhere do I discuss rehearsing on video. Although many disagree with me, my belief is that unless you are going to appear on video, you shouldn't rehearse on video. It is more important that you lose your self-consciousness and concentrate on engaging your audience than that you worry about which is your best side.

We tend to have a love/hate relationship with mirrors. As most of us were raised believing pride to be sinful, admiring our image—at least in front of another—is taboo. It is permissible to shave or put on makeup with a mirror, but we feel self-conscious if caught taking longer than necessary. It is incredible how often the most extroverted client becomes inhibited when asked to check out a mannerism, posture, or expression at the mirror in front of me, but those glass mirrors are great reality checks for attainable goals. There are very few Elizabeth Taylors or Gregory Pecks in this world, and looking into a mirror searching for something you're not is a waste of time. What you want to see reflected in a mirror is an inviting personality, someone who is able to move with confidence and who has no off-putting mannerisms. You want to practice at a mirror to see if you're getting close to your goals.

5) Rehearse as if there's an audience present. If you become too addicted to the mirror, when you do find yourself in front of a real audience, your best friend (your face in the mirror) won't be there to reassure you. Be like the cat who quickly becomes bored with his own image. Perform the presentation as if you are doing it for real. Rehearse the lines with the inflections you wish them to have. Practice the eye contact. As you practice aloud, make certain you move your head around the room. Just as posture is not static, neither should you be. The right amount of movement helps to keep an audience awake. A static speaker who appears frozen in place causes an audience's eyes to get extremely tired. However, to move does not mean to weave, pace, or wander. Nor should you move as you are making your point. You may, however, walk as you build up to the point you wish to get across, but you must stop walking when you get to the point you wish to make. You lose power when you move. When you do stop, make certain your weight remains on the back foot. Leaving the weight on your forward foot puts you in jeopardy of falling forward. Practice your hand movements until they become natural.

Impromptu Presentations

I am often asked about how to prepare for impromptu presentations. My answer: Practice them. No, I'm not being facetious. It's like a party game. Take a big bowl. Have as many people as you can fill out cards with ideas for a presentation: a toast, an announcement, a description of a trip you took, subjects that pertain to work, whatever. Each morning, pull one out and spend a few minutes trying to decide on a main theme; a beginning, middle, and end; with the close being the most important. Then try to deliver it out loud. I promise that within a few months you'll get really good at it.

So, once more: Rehearsals—the correct kind—will not, I repeat, WILL NOT make you stale. Staleness comes from rehearsing by rote. Rehearsing as if you're performing will turn you into a confident presenter; and once again: Confidence sells.

CHAPTER 10

Misconception: "Easy for you."

We've come to the last of the misconceptions. A misconception that comes up more often in looks than in words. I usually see it cross the faces of clients—even some of my own audiences—when I ask them to try something new and then show them how it's done. "Easy for you to do," their expressions say. "This is what you do for a living. Easy for you." Not to sound like a parent who survived the depression, but at one time, speaking in public was anything but easy for me. As a matter of fact, there was nothing that horrified me more.

In high school I could not speak when called upon. I would stand, open my mouth, and nothing would come out—something my clients and audiences have a hard time believing. Yet in those days, getting my thoughts organized in my brain so that they could travel in some reasonable order to my mouth and then to another soul was anything but easy for me. I could, however, perform onstage—the larger the audience, the better. As long as I could use somebody else's words, preferably song lyrics, I was fine. Asked to speak as myself, I'd freeze. No amount of acting training changed that. In fact, my dread of speaking up in group situations only increased after I graduated from one of the prime acting schools in the country. It got so bad that eventually, if I found myself in a group in which we were asked to introduce ourselves one by one, by the time my turn would arrive, I'd experience a wave of panic that would cause my voice to shake, my face to turn red, my heart to pound, and my mind to go blank. Only a dogged refusal to sucumb would keep me from passing out entirely.

By now, I would expect that you the reader might be wondering how, and more importantly why, someone would enter a field that required her to do the very thing she feared the most. It sounds crazy, if not downright idiotic, but in all honesty I didn't think that speaking in public would be part of the job description. I rather naively assumed that I could stay behind the scenes and use all the acting, voice, and dance training that I had amassed over the years to teach and direct others. I had done just that when I had worked in advertising, successfully directing actors and nonactors in radio commercials. It seemed perfectly logical to me that I could easily transfer my skills to people in business. Of course, I managed to overlook the most important aspect of doing business, which is: bringing the business in. That, as it turned out, required me to go in front of audience after audience and, to use show biz vernacular, strut my stuff. All by myself I'd managed to pick a field in which the adage about those who can, do, and those who can't teach, did not apply. In order to become a respected professional in my chosen field, I would have to not only do, but also be able to do it as well, if not better, than anyone else. Not to mention the fact that if I were to survive emotionally, I would have to begin to enjoy speaking in public, or my days and nights would be, to say the least, hell.

Enjoy! Now that's not a word often associated with speaking in public. As I have previously stated, public speaking leads the list of our worst fears. I knew I could call on all my previous training to provide me with whatever skills were needed to make a solid presentation, but that spark, that sense of enjoyment, that wanting to take the stage, all that draws audiences to speakers, had better be there, or my client list would be nil.

Most people who come for assistance with their presentation skills describe their difficulties in terms of audience and audience size, as touched upon in chapter 2. Some people prefer a small cluster of peers, while others experience their greatest discomfort when they face those they know—or more to the point, those who they suspect know them all too well. Some prefer to address a large group of friends, others a small group of unknowns. Some people react to the presence of an authority figure by enjoying the challenge of winning over the boss, while others find the real or perceived threat of an evaluation daunting. What it all comes down to is a matter of ego. While some may need the bolstering up of one or more friendly faces, others will prefer to perform to an anymous mass. I was of this last group.

In order to explain how I turned my problem around, I must make a small digression into the actor's world. Although this will be a rather broad generalization, basically, in the Western world, there are two forms of acting: one in which the actor works from the outside in (usually called the British school), and the other in which the actor works from the inside out (the so-called Method School of acting brought over from Russia by Konstantin Stanislavsky). To oversimplify the difference between the two methodologies, working from the outside in basically means finding the character you are to play in exterior mannerisms and uncovering the character layer by layer until you make the part your own. Working from the inside out means that you first search for yourself in the character and slowly develop the character's mannerisms, working from that core structure. Nowadays, with both English and American actors cross-pollinating, so to speak, by working together in films and onstage, there appears to be less of a delineation between the two, with each taking from the other. Where the truly great actors are concerned, the end result is the same. The part and the actor become one until they are indelibly etched in our minds. Olivier as Hamlet, Vanessa Redgrave as Lillian Hellman, Brando as Kowalski, Streep as Sophie.

One additional digression: Performers differ from actors in that whereas actors seek to become a character, performers remain themselves or the self they have created, no matter what the role. Debbie Reynolds is Debbie Reynolds, or at least the Debbie Reynolds she wishes to present to the world, no matter what role she's playing. Here again, talent can blur the lines. I am sure if you got a group of actors together they might differ as to who they put in which category. Julie Andrews: Actor? Performer? Or both? End of digression.

The reason I've gone into this the actor's jargon is that, in retrospect, in order to overcome my own fears of speaking in public, I simultaneously worked outside in and inside out to develop the character I wanted to become—the consummate speaker and teacher of presentation skills. Put another way, I pretended until I was.

From the outside in, I donned the wardrobe of the successful entrepreneur. I spent a fortune on my hair, makeup, clothes. Even if I wasn't yet the part, I'd be damned if I wouldn't look it. I never left the house—not even on days off—without every hair and stitch in place. I worked on my posture, honed my enunciation, and returned to practicing voice exercises that I'd thought I'd left way behind. I wrote my brochure, rewrote, and then rewrote it again until it looked as if it had been created by someone who knew the business. After six months of showing change after change to various professional writers, marketing mavens, and potential client types, I sent it off to the one person I'd been saving for last. Oh, how convinced I was that I'd get a gold star for my effort. Back came his fax: "Passive verbs suck. Rewrite!" I did.

From the inside out was much harder. I had to take

a cold hard look at all of my own misconceptions, especially those that concerned other people's realities. I still worry that I put my very first client in a strait-jacket for life because I was so concerned about showing off what I knew that I critiqued her to death rather than give her what she needed, wanted, and could take. I had to learn new techniques to master my own fears. I truly had to take to heart what I told clients, and I had to try each technique out for myself until I was certain it worked, and I had to watch client after client get that wonderful look on their face, that look that clearly said, "Easy for you to say, easy for you to do" every time I asked them to try something new. For a long, long time I couldn't tell them that it was anything but easy for me. Not until I developed true confidence in my own abilities and felt that my techniques were flawless, could I tell them that everything they watched me do was learned the hard way. The more the internals took hold, the more I could ease up on the externals. The hairstyle softened, and on days off I could be seen wearing jeans; my look relaxed.

Then there was the night I was to talk to a hundred women in business, and, because the woman in charge had forgotten to send out invitations, only the nine board members showed up—all of whom had no intention of leaving without the information they had been promised. Dinner took place on a dais with the ten of us munching away while we looked out at empty tables and idle waiters. Afterward, as I walked around the table to face the audience, I had all I could do to keep from breaking up. My mind kept flashing back to *The Mary Tyler Moore Show* episode in which

Ted Baxter opens a school, rents a huge hall, talks the "gang" into standing in as teachers, and has only one student register—a student who demands his money's worth. Mary et al. are forced to take the podium and lecture to an audience of one. In my case, my audience sat on the podium and I was the lone figure lecturing to the audience. I still find the story delicious. That evening was a milestone, as it showed me exactly how far I had come. Here I was in the most difficult and ludicrous of circumstances, in front of an audience of a size that at one time would have been the one I'd dreaded the most, and I was able to enjoy myself and the craziness of the situation. I knew then that if I could do it, anybody could. I also knew that what I had been telling my clients really worked. It was quite a high.

Martha Graham used to exhort her dancers to "take the dare" as they leapt across the floor. She urged them to risk the possibility of falling flat on their faces in exchange for the greater possibility of leaping out of the bounds of gravity. It was her way of saying that if you do not reach beyond yourself, you will not grow. I paraphrase her as I begin each of my workshops on personal communication skills. "This," I say, "is a place to fall on your face. A place to make a fool of yourself." It's usually too early in the day for the participants to feel comfortable enough to respond verbally, but their expressions say it all: "Easy for you to say. This is what you do for a living. Easy for you." I answer their looks aloud: "Everything you have seen and will see me do is learned behavior. I was not born knowing how to make eye contact, modulate my voice, read an audience as I speak, or have a wonderful time when I speak to audiences of any size." I can tell you, the reader, that as you master each of the techniques laid out in this book, it will become easier and easier and easier. More to the point, you will discover, as so many of my clients have, that speaking in public can be exhilarating, confidence giving, and an incredible amount of fun. So, begin. You'll end up having a ball. Promise!

Appendix:
Exercise Review

Chapter 3: Eye Contact

1) Intent. Remember, your intention is to ascertain *if and how* your listeners are taking in the information—not how they are taking in you.

2) Exercise.

1) Get a box of solid white notebook paper reinforcements and stick them in pairs around the room to represent the eyes of an audience. Put two on a lamp, two more on the wall, two more on books in the book shelf, and so on.

2) Using the sentence "Good morning! My name is _____ and yours is . . . ?" begin saying the first syllable to the first set of "eyes," skip over to the other side of the room for the second syllable, then to another set of eyes for the third syllable.

Keep going until the sentence is finished. Move slowly enough so that each sound of the syllable is pronounced.

Important: Do not leave a pair of eyes before the last sound of the syllable has been fully made. Practice taking a beat before you leave to go on to the next pair of eyes. You might want to ask someone to watch you as you practice the exercise to make certain that you do not inadvertently leave a pair of eyes before you have finished the last sound of the syllable.

3) As you progress, practice with two syllables, then three, then four.
4) Once you've mastered the above, practice alternating between words and phrases.

Keep in mind that passing your eyes over an audience or moving in the midst of a word or thought is like passing a tray of food around a cocktail party and not letting anyone get a morsel. The idea here is to watch your audience "swallow" your words.

Be certain that you don't move in consecutive order around the room. This practice of moving in a pattern becomes predictable, and your audience knows when to expect you to land on them, which inadvertently allows them to wander off mentally. It is best to reach out to the person farthest from you first, to the person nearest you second, then back again to the far side, then to the near side, working your way through the middle (see diagram on next page).

```
    5      20      1      21      3
      14   10              19    7
        8          17          13
     22       16        9         15
          13         12        23
      8         14         6
          2    11         18     4
```

You

Diagram

Chapter 4: Combating Nervousness

The Goal: to perform this exercise without anyone knowing that you are doing anything at all.

1) Sit in front of a mirror.
2) Keep your hands relaxed on your knees, your toes relaxed in your shoes.
3) Breathe throughout.
4) Squeeze all the muscles in your body from the collar bone down, except for your hands, toes, and those muscles you breathe with, including the stomach.
5) Hold for five seconds. Then relax. Make certain that you cannot see either the tightening or the relaxation in process.
6) Wait five seconds and repeat.

Check your facial expression. Your face should remain

animated. No staring. The last thing you wish to do is look as if you are on the potty. Do not mentally withdraw from the room. As you control your body muscles, your face must remain expressive.
Variations:

1) Once you've mastered the exercise sitting, try it standing.
2) Try tightening and relaxing a few muscles at a time.
3) See if you can talk while tightening and relaxing the basic muscles.
4) Try carrying on a conversation while tightening only selected muscles.

Practice this exercise in meetings, over breakfast or dinner, on the train, walking down the street.
Practice this when you're not nervous so you'll be able to use it when you are!
Remember: At the first signs of nervousness, don't panic! Butterflies simply show that you're alive and well with energy to harness. At the first signs of nervousness, start the exercise.

Chapter 5: The Strawberry

Part 1

1) Look into a mirror. Try to contract the eye muscle. One method: Grin from ear to ear until you find

yourself squinting the outer portion of the eye muscle; keep the eye muscle squinted and slowly allow the grin to leave the rest of your face. If the eye muscle drops, try again.

2) Repeat until you are able to maintain the squinted muscle without the grin. Once you've achieved this, you have activated the muscle.

Part 2

Close your eyes and think about someone you love or something you love to do. It could be your favorite food, a trip you took, making a hole in one or, of course, sex. Don't worry; even if someone is in the room with you, none of us can read minds, so enjoy your thoughts. Again, it makes no difference what you think about as long as you're energized eventually. When you feel thoroughly turned on, open your eyes and make certain your feelings are reflected in the mirror.

Search for a turn-on that will work for you consistently. Do not become concerned if the turn-on you've chosen doesn't show on your face. Often what we assume lights our fire may not produce the desired visual result. When you find your particular turn-on you should feel a small wave of electricity pulsate through your veins.

Chapter 6: Presentation Analysis Form

(Tear out and enlarge.)

MARGO T. KRASNE'S "SAY IT WITH CONFIDENCE"
PRESENTATION ANALYSIS FORM page 1

1	2A	2B
AUDIENCE DESCRIPTION	**AUDIENCE MOTIVATED BY:**	**AUDIENCE MOTIVATED BY:**
Who? How many?	What are your audience's **professional** "carrots" ?	What are your audience's **personal** "carrots" ?

3	4	5
WHAT YOU WISH YOUR AUDIENCE *TO DO*.	**YOUR STRATEGY (CONCEPT)**	**YOUR STRATEGY (PROOF)**
What you want your audience to do AFTER you've finished speaking	Use audience's "carrots" to entice toward your "to do."	Visuals Case histories

6	7
THEME	**TONE**
A theme runs through a presentation. For instance: your strategy your "to do" an analogy or . . .	For instance: upbeat, serious, urgent, warning, excited

8
YOUR TOPIC
OVERALL VIEW of CONTENT

THEME

PERSONAL REMINDERS

**SMILE
ENERGY POSTURE**

OPENING

There are no rules.
Possible openings:
your "to do,"
your theme

POINT

1st SUPPORT POINT

2nd SUPPORT & TRANSITION

POINT

1st SUPPORT POINT

2nd SUPPORT & TRANSITION

POINT

1st SUPPORT POINT

2nd SUPPORT & TRANSITION

CONCLUSION

YOUR "TO DO" or
REITERATION
OF THEME.

Chapter 7: Developing Good Hand and Arm Control

1) Use hands to express or emphasize a thought.
2) Keep hands away from crotch (the fig leaf position).
3) Keep hands in front of body.
4) Keep hands (either one or both) within your audience's peripheral vision of your face.
5) Feel your fingers, hands, and arms.
6) Practice with weights, soup cans, glasses filled with a few ice cubes.
7) Use mirror to try out what looks good.

Improving Speech Quality:

Use a tape recorder to check that you've pronounced each sound.

1) Put five fingers in mouth.
2) Keep your teeth off your fingers.
3) As loud as you can, enunciate each sound of each syllable:

THIS IS A REAL-LY DIFF-I-CULT EX-ER-CISE TO PER-FORM, BUT E-VEN-TU-AL-LY I WILL GET IT.

4) Repeat using any written copy.

Breathing:

1) Wear nonconfining clothing for all breathing exercises.

Lie on back on the floor, couch, or a firm mattress.

2) Place one hand on your diaphragm and one on your chest.

3) Breathe in slowly through your nose. Expand your stomach as if it were a balloon.

   Hand on chest should not move.

4) Exhale through your mouth. Your abdomen should sink in.

   Keep trying until it does. Again, do not move your chest.

   Do not go on until this is mastered.

5) Repeat steps 1–4, counting silently as you go.

   Take in as much air as possible.

   When you have reached your limit, press in with your palms in order to push out the air that is left.

6) Repeat step 5. This time, push stomach up toward the ceiling as you let out a loud strong "AH." Keep your throat open.

7) Work toward: four *slow* counts on inhale; eight *slow* counts on exhale.

   Concentrate on:

1) Making sure the diaphragm is moving in the right direction.

2) Regulating your counts.

3) Keeping throat and jaw relaxed at all times.

When this is mastered try doing it sitting up, then standing.

BIBLIOGRAPHY

Becker, Ernest. *The Denial of Death.* New York: The Free Press, 1973.

The Bible. Proverbs 16:18. Authorized St. James Version. London: Eyre & Spottiswoode Ltd., New York: Harper Brothers Publishers.

Bowlby, John. *Attachment and Loss.* Vol. 1, Part 4, *Ontogeny of Human Attachment.* New York: Basic Books, 1982.

Bugelski, B. R. *The Psychology of Learning Applied to Teaching.* Indianapolis: Bobbs-Merrill, 1971.

Carnegie, Dale. *How to Win Friends and Influence People.* New York: Pocket Books, 1936.

Carson, Robert C., and James N. Butcher. *Abnormal Psychology and Modern Life,* 9th edition. New York: HarperCollins, 1992.

Colthran, Tom. "TheValue of Visuals." Presentation Technologies Supplement to *Training* 6 (July 1989).

Cook, Blanche Wiesen. *Eleanor Roosevelt.* Volume 1, 1884–1933. New York: Viking Press, 1992.

Crystal, David. *The Cambridge Encyclopedia of Language.* Cambridge, England: Cambridge University Press, 1987.

Goffman, Erving. *The Presentation of Self in Everyday Life.* New York: Doubleday Anchor Books, 1959.

Goldberg, Carl. *Understanding Shame.* New Jersey: Jason Aronson, 1991.

Goleman, Daniel. *Vital Lies Simple Truths.* New York: Simon and Schuster, 1985.

Green, Ronald E. "Persuasive Properties of Color." *Marketing Communications,* October 1984.

Eisenberg, Arlene, Heidi E. Jurkoff, and Sandee Hathaway. *What to Expect the First Year.* New York: Workman, 1989.

Ekman, Paul, and Richard J. Davidson. "Voluntary Smiling Changes Regional Brain Activity." *Psychological Science* 4 (5). September 1993.

Ekman, Paul, W. V. Friesen, and M. O'Sullivan. "Smiles When Lying." *Journal of Personality and Social Psychology.* 1988.

Kohut, Heinz. *The Analysis of the Self.* New York: International Universities Press, 1971.

————. *The Restoration of the Self.* Connecticut: International Universities Press, 1977 (Reprinted 1993).

Kramer, Peter D. *Listening to Prozac.* New York: Viking, 1993.

Kupsh, Joyce. "The Effectiveness of Synchronized Sound Slide Packages in Beginning Typing." Unpublished doctoral dissertation, Arizona State University, Tempe, Arizona, 1975.

Leibowitz, Judith, and Bill Connington. *The Alexander Technique.* New York: Harper Perennial, 1990.

Levin, Jerome D. *Theories of the Self.* New York: Hemisphere, 1992.

Limerick, Patricia Nelson. "Dancing with Professors: The Trouble with Academic Prose." Essay adapted for *New York Times Book Review,* October 31, 1993 from speech given to Association of American University Presses, June 1993.

Mader, Sylvia S. *Inquiry Into Life,* 5th edition. New York: Wm. C. Brown, 1988.

Martin, Judith. *Miss Manners Guide to Excruciatingly Correct Behavior.* New York: Warner Books, 1983.

Mayer, Lyle V. *Fundamentals of Voice & Diction,* 10th edition. WCB Brown & Benchmark Publishers, 1994.

Myers, David G. *Pyschology,* 3rd edition. New York: Worth Publishers, 1992. Reprinted with permission.

The New Columbia Encyclopedia. William H. Harris and Judith S. Levey, eds. New York: Columbia University Press, 1975.

Peoples, David A. *Presentations Plus*, 2nd edition. New York: John Wiley & Sons, 1992.

Pinker, Steven. *The Language Instinct.* New York: William Morrow, 1994.

Reuter Textline Campaign, July 23, 1993. Headline: "UK: R.S. Alliance lands Pizza Base task as DMB &B bid falls flat."

Sarnoff, Dorothy, with Gaylen Moore. *Never Be Nervous Again.* New York: Crown, 1987.

Schad-Somers, Susanne P. *Sadomasochism: Etiology and Treatment.* New York: Human Sciences Press, 1982.

Shakespeare, William. Sonnet 116.

Stern, Daniel N. *The Interpersonal World of the Infant: A View from Psychoanalysis and Developmental Psychology.* New York: Basic Books, 1985.

Vogel, Douglas R., Gary W. Dickson, and John A. Leham. "University of Minnesota Persuasion and the Role of Visual Presentation Support: The UM/3M Study."

Wharton ARC. Applied Research Center, The Wharton School, University of Pennsylvania, September 14, 1981.

Williams, Margery. *The Velveteen Rabbit.* New York: Avon Books, 1975.

Winnicott, D. W. "Mirror Role of Mother and Family." In *Playing and Reality.* London and New York: Routledge, 1994.

Zimardo, Philip G. *Shyness*. Addison-Wesley Publishing Co., Inc., 1977.

Dictionaries

The American Heritage Dictionary of the English Language, 3rd edition. Houghton Mifflin Company, 1992.

The Compact Edition of the Oxford English Dictionary. Oxford University Press, 1985.

Langenscheidt's German-English Dictionary. K. G. Langenscheidt, Langenscheidt KG, 1993.

The Random House Dictionary of the English Language, The Unabridged Edition. Jess Stein, ed. Random House, 1967.

Webster's New Universal Unabridged Dictionary. Barnes & Noble Books, 1994.